I0155411

DANIEL
REDISCOVERED

THE TRUTH
WILL SET YOU FREE

C. S. MORRISON

QUALIAFISH

"The four beasts are usually understood by modern scholars to represent the Babylonian, Median, Persian and Greek empires respectively…It is not however easy to trace a special significance for every feature of each beast as an indication of the empire which it represents, and too much attention should probably not be given to such details…"

James Barr (Daniel 1962)

"The 2nd beast, **like a bear,** represents the Median Empire, which the author mistakenly believed had savagely torn at Babylon."

George A. F. Knight (The Book of Daniel, 1971)

"The bear as a symbol for the Median kingdom has most probably been chosen because of its known ferocity…and the dread it aroused…The statement that 'it was raised up on one of its sides and had three ribs in its mouth between its teeth' is obscure. There is probably here a cryptic allusion to Median greed for booty, while the bear's curious posture may imply aggressiveness rather than some kind of limitation of the effectiveness of the Medes as a power."

Norman W. Porteous (Daniel, 1965)

"The ten horns are kings of the Macedonian-Seleucid Empire, and to begin with the reference may have been indefinite, i.e. an actual prophecy from early Macedonian times…This procedure explains why it is rather difficult to fit the horns exactly and without doubt into the series of the kings."

James Barr (Daniel, 1962)

"It is usually held that the reckoning begins from the fall of Jerusalem…The words of the beginning of the reckoning in v.25 would seem in themselves rather to indicate the permission to rebuild Jerusalem…In any case the total number of years, 490, does not fit in with the chronology now known to us…"

James Barr (Daniel, 1962)

ABOUT THE AUTHOR

Colin S. Morrison is a science graduate and freelance philosopher with a lifelong interest in the book of Daniel. He gained his Masters degree in theoretical physics at the University of St Andrews in 1995, and currently lives in the UK, where he teaches mathematics. Puzzled by the incompleteness of the mainstream account of Daniel 7 and Daniel 9 (illustrated overleaf), and concerned that pressure from religious or anti-religious institutions has led scholars to misinterpret these passages, he has spent the last ten years examining the evidence to identify the view that a scientist under no such pressure would regard as most justified.

His conclusions about the book of Daniel differ radically from those of both critical and conservative scholars. Whilst accepting the mainstream (critical) viewpoint that *Daniel* was completed in the mid-160s BC, he argues that by far the most reasonable interpretation of Daniel 2, Daniel 7 and Daniel 9 is that these passages were included by the book's compiler to *predict the distant future of his own time* (their purpose being to counter skepticism about the book's authenticity). If so, they may well have come from a source that the compiler believed was a genuine seer. He points out that this possibility appears to be never considered by critical scholars despite the fact that Jewish readers in the 160s BC were *bound* to interpret these passages as predictions that were yet to be fulfilled. He also points out that the proposed compiler would have had *good reason* to include such predictions in a book of this nature. In view of this, he suspects that critical scholars are ignoring this possibility for fear that they might otherwise be labelled 'religious' or 'conservative'. In support of this conjecture he draws our attention to certain obvious pieces of evidence that he believes have been neglected in critical discussions of Daniel simply because they favour this 'prediction hypothesis'. And to demonstrate motive, he reveals just how stunningly accurate a portrayal of the rise of Christianity, and the end of Temple-based Jewish worship, emerges when these three prophecies are interpreted in their most justifiable way. He argues that, if this is no accident, critical scholars are doing the public a disservice by neglecting this very plausible explanation for their content.

"Daniel was in the greatest credit amongst the Jews,
till the reign of the Roman Emperor Hadrian:
and to reject his Prophecies, is to reject the Christian religion.
For this religion is founded upon his Prophecy
concerning the Messiah"

Sir Isaac Newton (1643-1727)

Preface

In Mark 13:14-20 Jesus Christ teaches his disciples:

[14]When you see the abomination of desolation spoken of by Daniel the prophet standing where it ought not (let the reader understand), then let those who are in Judea flee to the mountains... [19]For in those days there will be oppression such as there has not been the like from the beginning of creation... until now, and never will be. [20]Unless the Lord had shortened the days no flesh would have been saved. But for the sake of the chosen ones, whom he picked out, he shortened the days.

This passage is utterly fascinating. It also appears in Matthew 24 (and a greatly edited version makes it into Luke 21) so we can be quite certain of its antiquity. The fascinating thing about it is that it suggests that Christ knew the book of Daniel had been altered. And even better, it indicates that he regarded this as an act of mercy allowed by God that *does not ruin the book's prophetic role.*

Not one but two desolating abominations are mentioned in Daniel, one in Daniel 9:27 and the other in Daniel 11:31 and 12:11; and the latter is predicted to occur *hundreds of years before the former* (and two hundred years before Christ said these words). However, as Christ's words imply, that past abomination of desolation – a foreign idol installed at the Jewish Temple – was almost certainly *not predicted by Daniel the prophet*. It appears in a section of the book that has all the hallmarks of a piece of propaganda added to boost the morale of the Jewish faithful during a terrible persecution of their faith that happened in the 160s BC. Christ in the above passage even uses words *from this section of the book* to describe the *coming* persecution (which can only be the one hinted at in Daniel 9:27 and 7:25) as though he were returning these words to their original context. By saying that God 'shortened the days' of this coming oppression, he implies that those alterations to the book were done *for God's purposes*. What could this phrase mean other than that a prophecy or its context was altered so that the oppression seems far shorter than it will actually be? It can't mean God *changed his plans* as that would imply he miscalculated!

The duration of the coming oppression is given in Daniel 7:25 as 'a time, times and half a time'. And sure enough, we find this same phrase interpreted in Daniel 12:11 as a mere *3.5 years* – the true length of the oppression that *Daniel 12* refers to, but probably not the length of the worst oppression ever! As this book will show, when one ignores this ridiculous interpretation, the most justifiable meaning of that time phrase becomes 175 years, which is a much more respectable length for a time of hardship in Jewish history.

But the interpretations in Daniel 11-12 should only be ignored if they *are* ridiculous. The historical fulfilment of Daniel 11:31, for example, gives us the only indication in the Old Testament of what an abomination of desolation is. When we look for the next time in history when a foreign idol was permanently installed at the Jewish Temple site, we suddenly find that it was indeed followed by a time of hardship for all devout followers of Daniel's God that lasted exactly 175 years. And Christ was right! That oppression, or at least the first few years of it in Judea (Israel), was very probably *the worst oppression ever* judging from the huge slump in that country's population. The added sections of the book of Daniel thus seem to be acting as a key to ensure that careful readers only interpret these genuine prophecies in the way that history fulfilled.

While Daniel 12's three-and-a-half-year interpretation of the 'time, times and half a time' is a bit misleading if Daniel 7:25 was meant to predict an oppression lasting 175 years, God had good reason to make the latter seem much shorter. Daniel 7:26 says that soon after it God's people would receive the oppressor's kingdom. Had it not seemed almost over at its start, this could have been a big problem. As it was, they did receive that kingdom, but 176.5 years later – just one-and-a-half years after the oppression was *officially* ended!

Before I tell you about this book, I'd like to make it clear that I am an open-minded, scientific person, who is not committed to any prior doctrines on scripture, and who has no problem viewing biblical passages as exaggerations or fabrications included for propaganda and other purposes whenever the weight of evidence seems to favour that explanation for their content. The book of Daniel, the subject of this book, is no exception. Nevertheless, ever since I first read the book of Daniel I have suspected that there is something particularly special about that book. Having since then studied in detail what both critical and conservative scholars have written on it, I now believe I can show you exactly what that is.

Just as it claims, this twenty-seventh book of the Old Testament does contain objective evidence of the involvement of a God in human history. However, if you want to see this for yourself, you cannot simply accept what the book says at face value. You have to examine it in the same way critical scholars examine it. You need to look for the most justifiable explanation for the content of each passage it contains. And you must be prepared to accept that explanation (or at least acknowledge its likelihood) even if it seems at first to contradict your prior beliefs about the book's authorship.

If you are prepared to do this, then I will be able to show you what's special about Daniel. I should warn you, though: It will probably make you interested in Christianity. If you are a rational person like me who wants to hold the most scientifically justifiable worldview, what Christianity claims may well seem impossible – or at least highly unlikely. But don't let that put you off! One of the lessons of this book is that not all those claims are to be taken literally. I can assure you there are strong scientific reasons to believe in a God, and even grounds to expect that God to give us a message like that of Jesus. But for now, the important thing to remember is that the most reasonable explanation for an unexpectedly accurate prophecy is that it was written from hindsight. Only when that cannot possibly have been the case does one have grounds to invoke some other process to explain the occurrence of the predicted events. And only if these are unlikely to be the result of chance, or a consequence of the deliberate efforts of humans, have we any reason to postulate the involvement of any non-human intelligence. Only if we approach the prophecies in the book of Daniel in this scientific way can we expect to discover the objective evidence of God that I am claiming it contains.

As you will see in the first two chapters of this book, there is a lot of evidence in favour of the mainstream conclusion that the book of Daniel is a pseudonymous work, put together in the *second century BC* to bolster the morale of the Jews who were resisting a notorious attempt to stamp out their religion. The prophecies in Daniel 8 and 11 are ascribed to Daniel – a *sixth* century BC prophet – but were clearly intended to be understood as predictions of that persecution (and hence probably written then). A certain unfulfilled part of Daniel 11 is very reasonably explained as an attempt to make this last prophecy predict events that still lay in its writer's future, thus making the book seem more plausible. That is widely recognised. This book simply points out that a similar conclusion ought to apply to Daniel 2, Daniel 7 and Daniel 9:24-27 – a fact that critical scholars never mention. It shows that Jews in the second century BC would have understood these prophecies to also be *predictions of the future*. The reason critical scholars ignore this is probably because, as you will see in chapters 6-11, if they didn't, they'd have to admit that these prophecies were rather astonishingly fulfilled, and partly by the rise of Christianity.

Before we begin to examine these claims, I should also make clear that unlike the many critical and conservative scholars who have written about the book of Daniel, I am not committed to supporting the traditions of any academic institution or religious sect. Nor do I have any interest in ensuring my views conform to ones deemed acceptable to some peer group that I rely upon for positive reviews and publications. If my analysis of the book of Daniel had happened to show conclusive evidence of some non-Christian conception of God, or of merely human activity, I have no reason to cover this up. In writing this book, my only concern is that the views I put forward are the most justifiable ones – the ones best supported by the available evidence – and that they are communicated in as clear and accessible a way as I can manage.

That said, I am also not opposed to celebrating the extraordinary when one does encounter it – and as you will see, there are several fantastic examples in the book of Daniel. Instead of sweeping those instances of inexplicably accurate prophecy under the carpet just because they support the claims of a particular religion, I will be making every effort to inform the reader of their existence. I will thus be challenging the strange critical claim that the writer of Daniel 7 was not alluding to Alexander's four-part-divided Greek empire with his four-winged four-headed leopard, as all early readers of this book would have thought. I will also be opposing the ridiculous dogma that the writer of Daniel 6 intended his weak provincial ruler Darius the Mede – who is not allowed to deviate from *the law of the Medes and Persians* – to be thought of as a free Median *emperor*. Who ever heard of an emperor unable to cancel a decree he'd been tricked into issuing (especially one as unfavourable to him as an edict condemning his favourite minister to a nasty death)? And I am certainly not going to tell you to ignore the length of the time-periods that appear in Daniel 9:24-27.

Critical scholars only want you to do this so that you don't go looking at the history of the time this prophecy actually refers to. There you will see major historical events that fulfil all the predictions this prophecy makes, including the prediction that the Roman ruler who causes Jewish sacrifice and offering to cease will do so *in the middle of a seven-year period beginning with his re-founding of the city of Jerusalem and ending with his death.* In fact, you will see that when the "sevens" in this prophecy are interpreted in the way *most* justified by the text of Daniel, this seven-year period was very likely exactly one "seven" *to the day!*

They don't want you to notice this because that ruler's death is not the only event this prophecy predicts with such accuracy. Using the same meaning of "seven", you will find that the first sixty-nine "sevens" in the prophecy, which extend from 'the word to restore and rebuild Jerusalem' to the arrival of 'Christ', a king who will be put to death emptyhanded, reach precisely from the time Nehemiah received his permission to rebuild Jerusalem (early March 444 BC) to the likeliest date for the Triumphal Entry of Jesus – the most famous Christ of all. Again the precision could be *to the day!*

Since the amount of history one needs to cover in order to properly explain these prophecies may at times be hard for some readers to digest, I have kept it to the bare minimum. In particular, I have left out inessential names and dates, and avoided detailed discussions. There are, however, quite a few names and dates that do need to be mentioned. To help the reader see these in a wider historical context, I have listed them in chronological order on pages xvii-xviii. I have also summarised the content of the book of Daniel and some puzzling scholarly responses to it on pages xiii-xvi and xix-xxii. You might find it helpful to have a look at these pages first.

CONTENTS

TERMINOLOGY

Although commonly used to refer to the post-republican phase of Roman civilization, the term 'Roman Empire' is used in this book to denote the dominion of Rome from the time when she first began to conquer the surrounding city states, until the fall of Constantinople in 1453. In other words, it includes the Roman Republic. Where it is necessary to refer specifically to the post-republican phase, it will be called 'the rule of the Roman *Emperors'*.

For the Dominion of Rome up until Constantine's victory over Maxentius in 312 AD, I use the term 'Pagan Roman Empire'. Although the implication that following this event is the *Christian Roman Empire* is undoubtedly an oversimplification, this terminology does highlight the turning point in the fortunes of Christianity that this event definitely did constitute.

In line with the writer of the book of Daniel, I shall refer to the Macedonian Empire of Alexander the Great and his successors as the *Greek Empire (*or just *Greece)*, the historical Persian (Achaemenid) Empire of Cyrus the Great as the *Medo-Persian Empire*, and the Neo-Babylonian Empire of Nebuchadnezzar as the *Babylonian Empire.*

All ancient dates given will be Julian calendar dates unless otherwise indicated. Prior to 4 AD, they are technically 'proleptic Julian calendar' dates (dates obtained by extrapolating the Julian calendar back to cover dates prior to the date its leap-year system became fixed), but for simplicity the word 'proleptic' has been omitted.

Bible quotations are based on the WEB translation. However, where others differ significantly, a careful judgement has been made as to the most likely rendering. Verses in Daniel are sometimes abbreviated 'Dan' (e.g. Daniel 7:5 may also appear as Dan 7:5). Since the text of certain passages is discussed over several chapters of this book, I have begun each quotation with the abbreviated verse reference in underlined bold typeface. This will hopefully make it easy for the reader to look back at earlier parts of a passage, despite the fact that they are quoted in previous chapters. Quotations are indented on the left, and where comments have been inserted into a quotation they are enclosed in square brackets. All highlighting, whether bold, italic or underlined, is my emphasis.

BOOK OF DANIEL CHAPTER SUMMARIES

DANIEL 1: Setting the Scene (Language: *Hebrew*)

How Daniel was brought to Babylon by king Nebuchadnezzar, and how he received training in Babylonian culture along with three other talented young Hebrew men of noble birth and devout faith.

DANIEL 2: The Metal Statue Dream (Language: *Aramaic* from v.4)

King Nebuchadnezzar's overreaction to his dream of a dazzling metal statue, and the account and interpretation of that dream given by Daniel in exchange for the lives of the wise men of Babylon. The statue's *gold, silver, bronze* and *iron* parts stand for distinct empires.

DANIEL 3: The Fiery Furnace (Language: *Aramaic*)

How Daniel's three friends miraculously survive being thrown into a fiery furnace by king Nebuchadnezzar for refusing to worship a huge gold statue he had erected.

DANIEL 4: The Dream of a Tree (Language: *Aramaic*)

King Nebuchadnezzar's account of his dream of a luscious tree ordered to be chopped down by heavenly beings and reduced to a stump whose heart is to be replaced for '7 times' with an animal's, Daniel's interpretation, and the ensuing madness, which fulfilled the interpretation. The king claims it to be a judgement of the Jewish God for his pride, and that it only abated when he looked to heaven and acknowledged God's supreme authority and his own humanity.

DANIEL 5: The Writing on the Wall (Language: *Aramaic*)

The account of Babylonian King Belshazzar's Feast, the creepy disembodied fingers the king sees writing on the wall, and Daniel's pessimistic but true interpretation which was fulfilled that very night by Darius the Mede's capture of Babylon and killing of Belshazzar.

DANIEL 6: Daniel in the Lions' Den (Language: *Aramaic*)

How Daniel, having risen in status, miraculously survives being thrown to the lions on the reluctant orders of King Darius the Mede for refusing to obey an anti-Jewish decree the king had been tricked into issuing by governors jealous of Daniel's success.

DANIEL 7: **The Four Monsters Dream**   (Language: *Aramaic*)

Daniel's dream of four beasts that are four empires: A winged *lion*, a lopsided *bear* with three ribs in its mouth, a four-winged four-headed *leopard,* and a terrifying eleven-horned unnamable *monster*.

DANIEL 8: **The Ram and Goat Vision**   (Language: *Hebrew*)

Daniel's vision of a ram and a goat representing the conquest of the Medo-Persian Empire by Alexander the Great, and the subsequent rise of the Greek Seleucid kingdom and its anti-Semitic king Antiochus Epiphanes, who tries to abolish the Jewish religion.

DANIEL 9: **The Seventy 'Sevens' Prophecy**   (Language: *Hebrew*)

Daniel's confessional prayer for Jerusalem, and the remarkable vision and prophecy of the city's future that he received in response.

DANIEL 10: **Daniel's vision of 'a man'**   (Language: *Hebrew*)

The vision of a hovering, linen-clad angel with fiery eyes and thunderous voice, which introduces the book's long final prophecy.

DANIEL 11: **The Syrian Wars Prophecy**   (Language: *Hebrew*)

Prophecy of the wars between the Seleucids and Ptolemies which culminates in a prediction of Antiochus Epiphanes' deeds and death.

DANIEL 12: **The End**   (Language: *Hebrew*)

Prediction of the length of the coming persecution, and divine glory and eternal life for those who stand firm in the face of it.

Since this book is concerned with the long-term prophecies in the book of Daniel it focusses almost exclusively on Daniel 7-12 and Daniel 2 (much of which will be quoted in the text). The other chapters will only be mentioned when their content is relevant for the purpose of determining the most justifiable interpretation of these prophecies. Nevertheless, the reader may be interested to note that the message of the tales that have been included in Daniel 3, 4, 5 and 6 (the power of the Jewish God over earthly kings, and his ability to rescue his faithful from seemingly inescapable death) is highly consistent with the purpose of the book that we will identify in chapter 2.

TABLE OF DREAM IMAGERY IN DANIEL 2, 7 & 8

DANIEL 2 *(ch.10)*	**DANIEL 7** *(ch.8-9, 11-13)*	**DANIEL 8** *(p.121)*
Gold Head of huge metal statue =Nebuchadnezzar **=BABYLON**.	**Lion with Eagle's wings** made to look like a man and given a man's heart (=Dan. 4) =Nebuchadnezzar**=BABYLON**.	*Although set in the Babylonian period, this vision does not depict Babylon.*
Silver Chest and Arms ='inferior' kingdom to follow Babylon (though *all 3 other parts* have metals that imply inferiority to Babylon).	**Two-sided Bear** which has *one side **higher** than the other* and *three ribs in its mouth between its teeth.* It is told to 'Get up and devour much flesh!'	**Two-horned Ram** with *one horn **higher** than the other* (it also grew up later) =the empire of the **MEDES AND PERSIANS**.
Bronze Belly and Thighs =third kingdom: A kingdom that will *'rule over all the earth'* (including all Greece!).	**Leopard** that has *4 wings* (like a bird's) and *4 heads.* It is *'given power to rule'*. (Could this mean its kings didn't *inherit* such power?)	**One-horned he-goat** =**GREECE** [Alexander]. It flies over all earth, slaughtering the ram. Horn=1st king snaps. *4 horns* replace it. *4 horns=4 kingdoms not ruled by the first king's descendants.*
Iron Legs with Iron-and-clay Feet =fourth kingdom – strong as iron since it *breaks up* many others, but latterly weaker due to divisions that won't be fixed by intermarriage, and may even be caused by it.	**Mighty and *distinct* Beast,** =kingdom *unlike all before it.* It bites with *large iron teeth,* and crushes with *bronze claws.* It has 10 horns=10 kings. *A little 11th uproots 3 of them,* thickens, gains mouth & eyes, speaks against the Most High, defeats the holy people and tries to change times and law. They are his for 3.5 *times.*	A little horn grows out of one of the four getting very tall and blasphemous. It casts down a few stars and defiles the Temple. It is a king who will oppress Israel in the *latter time* of the Greeks [=Epiphanes]
Stone from *a mountain, cut out without hands,* strikes the statue's feet, shattering it all to dust, and becomes *a mountain filling the whole earth.* =Eternal kingdom to be set up during the time of the 4th empire's kings.	A heavenly council convenes. **One like a son of man comes** who is honoured by God. **He gets an eternal kingdom and worship by all nations.** The beast is killed and burned. **Others stay alive for a while.** Holy people gain a kingdom, and will possess it forever.	After 2300 evenings and mornings the Temple is cleansed, and God will then break that evil king. *No fourth empire or eternal kingdom features in Daniel 8.*

TABLE OF ACCEPTED HISTORY IN DAN 8 AND 11

DANIEL 8   *(p.121-2)*

- Portrays a time of Persian (Medo-Persian) dominance followed by the conquest of the Persian Empire by the 'first king' of 'Greece' (Alexander the Great).

- Portrays Alexander's death and how his Greek empire would split into four separate weaker kingdoms ruled by people who were not Alexander's descendants.

- Portrays the illegitimacy and fateful rise of Antiochus IV Epiphanes, and how he would oppress the Jews and defile their Temple. It then predicts a cleansing of the temple and his death.

DANIEL 11   *(p.10, 127-8, 123-5)*

- Correctly states that the fourth king to rule the Persian empire after Cyrus – Xerxes I – would be exceedingly wealthy and use his riches to 'stir up everyone against Greece', and that a 'mighty king' (Alexander the Great) would rise (150 years later in fact, but causally linked).

- Portrays same four-way split of Greek Empire. It then focuses on two of these four kingdoms: the Seleucid state to the north of Israel, and the Ptolemaic empire centred in Egypt (the south). These two kingdoms fought six wars over Syria and Palestine, called the *Syrian Wars*–to follow:

- Portrays the rise of Seleucus I (originally a general in Ptolemy I's army) and alludes to the marriage of Berenice, daughter of Ptolemy II, to the 3rd Seleucid king Antiochus II, which sealed the peace treaty after the *second* Syrian war.
- Suggests the intrigue that led to Berenice's murder, and the *third* Syrian war, in which her brother Ptolemy III tried to destroy Seleucus II.
- Portrays Ptolemy III's very successful punitive campaign, and Seleucus II's aborted response.
- Describes the later invasion by Seleucus II's son Antiochus III starting the *fourth* Syrian war, and his costly defeat by Ptolemy IV at Raphia.
- Alludes to Antiochus III's later victory over Ptolemy V at Panium, his daughter's marriage to Ptolemy (which ended the *fifth* Syrian war), and his catastrophic defeat by Rome in 189 BC.
- Briefly alludes to his subsequent death and the reign and assassination of his son Seleucus IV.

- Portrays the illegitimate rise of Antiochus IV Epiphanes, his conquest of Egypt (in the *sixth* Syrian war), his return a year later, and Rome's decisive intervention that forced his withdrawal. It then describes his acts against the Jews, and...
...predicts an *unknown* Seleucid attack on Egypt and the victorious king's death near Jerusalem.

LIST OF RELEVANT HISTORICAL EVENTS

70-YEAR PERIOD OF *BABYLONIAN* DOMINANCE

609 BC: **Fall of Assyria. Babylon rises to dominance** in alliance with Media.
605 BC: Nebuchadnezzar becomes king of Babylon. Babylon defeats Egypt.
603 BC: Daniel interprets Nebuchadnezzar's dream of four empires (Daniel 2).
587 BC: Nebuchadnezzar destroys Jerusalem and her Temple.
553 BC: Belshazzar made coregent in Babylon with his father Nabonidus.
553 BC: Daniel dreams of four monsters representing four empires (Daniel 7).
551 BC: Setting of Daniel 8 (Daniel's 'ram and goat' vision of Persia & Greece)
550 BC: Cyrus of **Persia** seizes the Median throne (but spares the Median king).
546 BC: Cyrus conquers Lydia but spares the life of its king Croesus.
539 BC: **Cyrus' Medo-Persian forces conquer Babylon** (sparing Nabonidus).

208-YEAR PERIOD OF *MEDO-PERSIAN* DOMINANCE

539 BC: Setting of the 'Seventy 'Sevens'' Prophecy in Daniel 9.
538 BC: Cyrus lets the Jews return to rebuild their temple.
536 BC: Setting of Daniel 11 (Daniel's 'prophecy' of the *Syrian wars*).
525 BC: Persia under Cyrus' son Cambyses conquers Egypt.
509 BC: Founding of the Roman Republic.
490 BC: Greeks repel invading Persian force at battle of Marathon.
480 BC: Greeks defeat Persian fleet at Salamis and later win on land at Plataea.
444 BC: Artaxerxes I of Persia gives Nehemiah permission to rebuild Jerusalem.
396 BC: Fall of Italian city of Veii to Roman forces. Rome begins to rise.
331 BC: **Alexander the Great of Macedon and Greece conquers Persia.**

141-YEAR PERIOD OF *GREEK* DOMINANCE

327 BC: Alexander the Great invades and conquers part of India.
323 BC: Alexander the Great dies unexpectedly in Babylon.
311 BC: Empire splits in four: *Egypt, Asia, Thrace* (later *Pergamon*), *Macedon*.
304 BC: Ptolemy I becomes king of *Egypt*, and Seleucus I king of *Asia*.
281 BC: Seleucus I conquers *Thrace*. Attalid dynasty seizes power at *Pergamon*.
277 BC: Antigonus II establishes Antigonid dynasty of kings at *Macedon*.
261 BC: Eumenes I establishes Attalid independence at *Pergamon*.
252 BC: Marriage of Antiochus II to Berenice ends second Syrian war.
246 BC: Ptolemy III mounts successful punitive war against Seleucus II.
217 BC: Battle of Raphia: Ptolemy IV defeats Antiochus III.
200 BC: Battle of Panium: Antiochus III defeats the forces of Ptolemy V.
189 BC: **Rome defeats Seleucid king Antiochus III to dominate the world.**

188 BC: Peace of Apamea: Rome secures vast tribute from Seleucid Empire.
175 BC: Death of Seleucus IV: Antiochus Epiphanes seizes Seleucid throne.
171 BC: Greek king Perseus of Macedon rebels against Rome.
169 BC: Antiochus Epiphanes conquers Egypt, but invades again the next year.
168 BC: Rome defeats Perseus, and the following year breaks up his kingdom.
168 BC: Rome orders Antiochus Epiphanes out of Egypt. He attacks the Jews.
167 BC: Temple defiled. Jews under Judas Maccabeus rebel against Epiphanes.
165 BC: **Book of Daniel completed around this time.**
164 BC: Judas liberates Jerusalem and rededicates the Jewish Temple.
164 BC: Epiphanes falls ill and dies whilst campaigning in Persia (Iran).
161 BC: Judas Maccabeus sends embassy to Rome.
160 BC: Judas dies fighting the Seleucids. His brothers continue the struggle.

82 BC: *Sulla* is made 'Dictator' in Rome *with no time limit imposed.*
63 BC: Roman occupation of Judea begun by Pompey.
44 BC: *Julius Caesar* accepts office of *Dictator for Life* and gets assassinated.
23 BC: *Augustus Caesar* granted tribunician *power for life* (consular in 19 BC)
13 AD: *Tiberius'* powers made equal to those of Augustus who dies in AD 14.
33 AD: Jesus of Nazareth crucified at Jerusalem (3rd April).
38 AD: Tiberius dies. His heir *Caligula* becomes emperor in his place.
41 AD: Caligula killed by Praetorian Guard who then make *Claudius* emperor.
54 AD: Claudius dies suddenly (probably poisoned). *Nero* is made emperor.
64 AD: Christians made scapegoats for a fire in Rome and suffer persecution.
66 AD: First Jewish revolt against Rome. Nero sends Vespasian to put it down.
68 AD: Galba rebels. Nero commits suicide. *Galba* becomes emperor.
69 AD: **'The Year of the Four Emperors'**. Galba-*Otho-Vitellius-Vespasian.*

70 AD: Jerusalem and her Temple are utterly destroyed by the Romans.
74 AD: Remaining Jewish rebels commit suicide at Masada.
93 AD: Josephus writes about the book of Daniel in *Antiquities of the Jews.*
115 AD: Tension between Jews and Romans erupts into widespread violence.
117 AD: Roman General Quietus finally puts down this Jewish 'Kitos' revolt.
130 AD: Emperor *Hadrian* promises the Jews he will rebuild Jerusalem.
131 AD: Aelia Capitolina (Hadrian's city) founded on top of Jerusalem's ruins.
132 AD: Second Jewish revolt against Rome led by Simon Bar Kokhba.
135 AD: Hadrian crushes Jewish revolt. His statue is set up on Temple Mount.
136 AD: Jews expelled from Palestine. Building of Jerusalem (Aelia) continues.
138 AD: Hadrian dies of disease on 10th July, seven years after founding Aelia.
303 AD: Emperor Diocletian begins the Great Persecution of Christians.
311 AD: Galerius' *Edict of Toleration* officially ends Persecution of Christians.
312 AD: **Constantine defeats Maxentius to be sole emperor in the West.**

SOME PUZZLES OF CRITICAL SCHOLARSHIP

STRANGE EQUATIONS

DARIUS THE MEDE = KING OF MEDIA: Why do critical scholars cite the Median ethnicity of the conqueror of Babylon in Daniel 5:31 and 9:1 as evidence that the writer of Daniel 7 mistakenly thought Babylon fell to Media rather than to the historical Medo-*Persian* empire, when in Daniel 6 that king rules according to 'the law of the Medes *and Persians*' – a law that he is *afraid to break?*

THE MOST HOLY (TO BE ANOINTED) = THE TEMPLE SANCTUARY: Why do mainstream scholars identify the 'Most Holy' *to be anointed* in Daniel 9:24 as *the Jerusalem Temple Sanctuary* when the very next verse speaks of an *Anointed One* who would be *put to death*, and who is therefore very obviously *a person*?

MISSING EQUATIONS AND INEQUALITIES

DANIEL 9 ≈ NEHEMIAH 1: Why don't critical commentaries on Daniel discuss the similarity of the prayer in Daniel 9 to the payer that is found in Nehemiah 1 – a prayer prayed by none other than Jerusalem's famous wall-builder Nehemiah and answered by his royal permission to rebuild Jerusalem (just as Daniel's prayer is answered by his *prophecy* of Jerusalem's rebuilding)?

ITALY > GREECE: Why do mainstream articles and commentaries on Daniel give the false impression that the power of Rome was relatively unknown to the Jews at the time Daniel was written, when the authors of these works must be fully aware that this was over twenty years *after* Rome famously and decisively conquered the Greek Seleucid Empire to dominate the Mediterranean?

GOAT = DIONYSUS = ALEXANDER THE GREAT: Why do experts in critical scholarship fail to emphasise that a goat may have been chosen in Daniel 8 to represent the Greek Empire of Alexander the Great because it was a popular symbol of the Greek *wine god,* Dionysus, with whom Alexander was often equated?

4 HEADS = 4 KINGDOMS = GREECE: Why do so few critical scholars acknowledge that the intended readers of Daniel were bound to identify the *four-headed leopard* in Daniel 7 as Greece? The leopard was, after all, another popular symbol of Dionysus, and the writer of the book of Daniel clearly perceived Alexander's Greek Empire as being **split into four Greek kingdoms**.

RAISED AND LOWERED SIDES = HIGHER AND LOWER HORNS: Why do so few scholars comment on the fact that the raised side and lowered side of the bear in Daniel 7 appear to be an exact analogy to the higher horn and lower horn of the ram in Daniel 8?

WORLD-RULING KINGDOM = GREECE: Why do most critical scholars think that *Persia*, the nation who was famously kicked out of Greece at the peak of her powers in 479 BC, would be regarded in the Greek world of 165 BC as the empire that will 'rule over all the earth' in Daniel 2:39?

DANIEL 2 & 7 = PREDICTIONS OF *CONQUEST* OF GREEK EMPIRE: On what grounds do scholars who claim that Daniel 2 and Daniel 7 were originally written as predictions of the Greek Empire's *longevity* exclude the possibility that they were actually designed to predict that empire's *overthrow by a more powerful gentile nation* – or even the *Roman* Empire's longevity?

FOURTH MONSTER = ROME: Why don't scholars ever consider the possibility that Daniel 7 was included as a prediction of the distant future to counter suspicions that the book of Daniel was a forgery?

UNRECOGNISABLE = DENIABLE: Why is the absence of explicit references to Rome in Daniel not assumed to be the result of diplomatic concerns (the possibility of offending a potential ally)?

LION, BEAR, LEOPARD, "?" = BABYLON, PERSIA, GREECE, ROME:

Why do experts in critical scholarship never seriously consider the obvious possibility that the writer of Daniel 7 intended the sequence of empires in his monster dream to be as above? Not only is this view convincingly supported by the corresponding symbolic imagery used for Persia and Greece in Daniel 8, but it was also fully accepted by all the ancient commentators up to Porphyry – and even *he* did not question the identity of the first *three* empires.

DANIEL 7 = REMARKABLY ACCURATE PORTRAYAL OF HISTORY:

Why do critical scholars fail to acknowledge the astonishing coincidence evident in the way the most straightforward reading of Daniel 7 (and Daniel 2) appears to accurately describe history as we know it? It is not as if they haven't noticed. Their straw-grasping claim that the writer of this prophecy mistakenly believed in a whole extra empire is a clear admission of its predictiveness.

A WINGED LION standing for Babylon is followed by a BEAR that has *ONE SIDE HIGHER THAN THE OTHER* and *THREE RIBS IN ITS MOUTH BETWEEN ITS TEETH*. This perfectly reflects the fact that Babylon was conquered by the *"two-sided" Medo-Persian Empire* (represented by a ram in Daniel 8 that has *'one horn higher than the other'*) – an empire whose founding king Cyrus was noted for sparing the lives of *three defeated emperors*.

That BEAR gets followed by a *FOUR-WINGED, FOUR-HEADED* LEOPARD, just as the Persian Empire fell to Alexander, whose Greek (Macedonian) Empire *split into four Greek kingdoms (four wings)* each ruled by the head of a distinct *dynasty (four heads)*.

There then arises a TEN-HORNED BEAST with *LARGE IRON TEETH, BRONZE CLAWS* and *AN ELEVENTH HORN THAT UPROOTS THREE OF ITS TEN HORNS*. It represents a terribly powerful and unique empire – *different from all previous ones* – from which would emerge a sequence of eleven kings. The eleventh of these would *subdue three of the first ten*, make war on devout followers of the Jewish God, and defeat them, and would also speak against their God. Sometime after this king, says the same passage, his empire will pass into the hands of devout followers of that same God (who will also serve a heavenly king described as 'one like a son of man' whose kingdom is 'eternal').

The emphasis on the greater power and total uniqueness of this fourth empire means that it can only be *consistently* interpreted as Rome (the subjugator of the four Greek kingdoms, and undeniably the ruling empire at the time the book of Daniel was completed). It is therefore utterly astonishing that the eleventh dictator to be granted an unlimited reign over the Roman Empire (the least arbitrary definition of its 'king') rose to power in a *"Year of the Four Emperors"* in which *the three previous unlimited dictators* were violently deposed and replaced in rapid succession! Even more remarkable is the fact that this eleventh unlimited dictator of Rome *fought against the Jews and defeated them*. His forces destroyed Jerusalem and its Temple in 70 AD. And he is also remembered for his use of divine omens – including a Jewish prophecy – to legitimise his comparatively weak claim to power.

Critical scholars may protest that this incredible accuracy only applies to one way of interpreting this passage. However, for reasons detailed in chapter 8 of this book, it is by far the most *justifiable* way – the way its writer almost certainly *intended* it to be understood. As such, this match with history is highly relevant to critical scholarship. It explains why the book of Daniel has fascinated so many intellectuals over the ages. Without it, for example, it would be hard to understand why the Romano-Jewish historian Josephus risked everything to claim that Daniel foretold the rise of Rome. Yet it never features in critical discussions. The reason is very probably the fact that it is near impossible for this passage to date from the first century AD. All the signs are that it was included in its current form as long ago as 165 BC to complete a piece of religious propaganda designed to boost the morale of the Jews at a critical moment in their nation's history. And as a result, its amazing accuracy *cannot be due to hindsight*.

1. Introduction

"Translate it for me!", the king demanded nodding at the scroll in the messenger's hand. The messenger bowed and cleared his throat nervously. The Macedonian king of Asia hadn't disguised his irritation on hearing the somewhat negative report this messenger had brought him from the southwest corner of his empire.

It was really only a very minor setback. A hint of revolt amongst the peasants in the Judean countryside. Jerusalem still lay firmly in his grip. Worship of Zeus continued to grace her temple; and her citizens were at least publicly implementing his reforms. However, the king clearly had assumed that the measures he'd taken were more than enough to convince the rebellious population that their god was no match for those of Greece. Not only had he slaughtered thousands who would not renounce their barbarous religion, he had also cleaned out their temple of its gold and silver and precious objects, forbade its traditional use, and raised an altar therein to Zeus, the father of the gods (Since the Jews only worshipped one god, the thunderbolt-wielding head of the Olympian pantheon was the only one of the true deities they seemed likely to accept).

At the same time, his soldiers had rendered the Judean capital indefensible by demolishing sections of her 280-year-old wall. To ensure she remained that way, he had built a fortress therein and installed his most trusted regiment with orders to enforce Greek customs. And he'd even organised a public display of Jewish submission. The Jerusalemites had been dressed in ivy and made to join the procession in honour of Dionysus. The ivy was a popular symbol of that youngest resident of Mount Olympus – the 'Good Deity' to whom the Greeks attributed the grape harvest, wine, and merriment. But in this king's eyes, it also signified the bonds of slavery and servitude that his people had imposed upon the Jews.

As everybody knew, the founder of his empire, Alexander, who had conquered the whole world for Macedon, was, if not the very incarnation of Dionysus, then at least the sword in Dionysus' hand. His mother adored that god, and Alexander was famous for wine-drinking and revelry. Most significantly, though, he had conquered India. That vast territory on the edge of the known world had, according to legend, been the conquest of Dionysus himself – a god who, when not making merry, made war. Dressed in leopard skins, he went to battle with a fearsome entourage of leopards, panthers and lions. Alexander was thus merely reclaiming India *for him*. And this eighth king of the Seleucid dynasty of Alexander's successors no doubt felt he was doing the same with Judea.

The diadem on the king's forehead glinted in the torchlight as he sat back expectantly while the messenger undid the leather straps of the scroll he bore. It was another reminder of the high esteem in which the Macedonians held their leopard-loving wine god. They attributed their success so much to Dionysus that they had even modelled their royal headgear on his famous *mitra* headband. A nagging image of the once-proud men of Judah reluctantly bound in ivy being led by laughing, leopard-clad, mitra-crowned Greeks briefly invaded the messenger's mind as he opened the scroll.

He had acquired it on one of his Sabbath raids. The Sabbath of the Jewish seven-day week was the most obvious day to comb the countryside for rebels. On that day they were very easy to spot. They offered no resistance, and would not do any work his soldiers commanded. He had found this scroll being read to an unexpectedly large gathering of villagers. Naturally he had ordered the ring leaders to be executed if they refused to publicly renounce their faith, and had instructed that their followers be flogged. He would usually have left it at that. However, on examining the contents of this scroll, it had quickly dawned on him that he wasn't looking at a religious text of the ancient sort he was so used to seeing and burning. This one seemed clearly of *recent* origin. Yet its allusions to recent events were so cleverly interwoven with material from ancient sources that the few prisoners he could persuade to talk were adamant they'd heard this book before. For them it was accurate prophecy. And it said that their people would survive this king and later rule the world. Thinking God was on their side, they'd been far less compliant. This was a change he had to report.

He looked down at the neat rows of Hebrew letters that had emerged and began to wonder whether he'd made the right decision. He had already explained the contents of the scroll to the king. However, he had tactfully left out the part of its final prophecy that alluded to this king's death. He had also omitted the bit about the ships of *Kittim*. The public humiliation this king had suffered at the hands of his one-time Roman friend Gaius Popilius Laenus, which this was clearly about, would still be a source of deep pain and anger. It had not only put paid to his hopes of ruling Egypt, but had made him look a fool in front of his whole army.

However, he felt certain the king lacked the patience to listen right through to the end. It was getting late, and he was confident he could drag out the earlier passages. The king was bound to be amused by their repeated prediction of Rome's demise at the hands of the Jewish God. He might even see this as an easy opportunity to boost his credibility in the eyes of those Italian king-makers. Having recently crushed the Jews, and all but wiped out their religion, he could easily claim to have saved Rome from that predicted fate. The Senate may well honour him for this – and at present he needed all the support in Rome that he could muster. The Romans still held his nephew, Prince Demetrius, whom many regarded as the rightful king. In their eyes this king was a mere usurper. If the Senate chose to back Demetrius, he was finished. Feeling better, he cleared his throat again and began to read aloud.

> "In the third year of the reign of Jehoiakim king of Judah Nebuchadnezzar king of Babylon came to Jerusalem and besieged it. The Lord gave Jehoiakim king of Judah into his hand, with some of the vessels of the house of God; and he carried them into the land of Shinar to the house of his god..."

Although about an event four hundred years earlier, the parallels with recent history in these opening lines were clear: Like king Nebuchadnezzar, this king had also robbed the Jewish Temple as one of his first acts against that nation. He had needed the money. His father's defeat by Rome had left a huge debt to pay, which the Romans were unlikely to forget. The messenger read on. The scroll next said that Nebuchadnezzar had financed the training of a Jew who later prophesied the downfall of his kingdom! Could one of this king's own agents in Judea perhaps see himself in such a role today? It then described the act that had brought this Jew to prominence: His interpretation of Nebuchadnezzar's second-worst nightmare – a dream predicting the demise of his kingdom. But it didn't just predict the fall of *his* kingdom. It predicted the overthrow of the one to follow his, and even the one to come after that. Thanks to Herodotus, everyone was well aware that Nebuchadnezzar's empire had fallen to the Persian armies of Cyrus. They also knew that, two hundred years later, the Persians were conquered by Alexander. Hence the only obvious possibility for the unnamed fourth empire – strong as iron – was Rome. The messenger recalled his surprise at the stubbornness with which even the older villagers insisted they'd heard this story *as children*.

The king looked bored. "Let's get to the important part!", he yawned, "Where do *I* come into it?..."

Although the above scenario is fictional, it does portray an event that could have occurred somewhere in the Middle East in the mid-160s BC in the run-up to a major turning-point in Jewish history known as the Maccabean Revolt when the Jews of Judea took on the vast Seleucid Empire, and ultimately won their freedom. The document being discussed – the text we now know as *the book of Daniel* – could actually have played a critical hidden role in that episode in history through its effect upon the morale of its early readers. But as you will see, that is not its most interesting feature.

In this short book I'm going to make some surprisingly obvious, and seemingly very significant, observations about the content of the book of Daniel. As you will discover, those observations are not obscure or difficult to understand. Nor are they trivial details that have little bearing on the question of the origin and purpose of that Old Testament book. Indeed, it is these observations that directly give rise to my introductory puzzles (pages xix-xxii) – questions that suggest the content of certain passages in that book is not being interpreted in the most justifiable way. Yet these observations are inexplicably absent from critical discussions of Daniel. In fact, having read lots of articles on Daniel written by expert scholars I am quite convinced that these observations have not been made before, or, if they have been, they have not received the academic attention that they very clearly deserve. The reason they are so important is because they indicate that the consensus which mainstream scholars have reached about the content of the book of Daniel is only half true. In fact, they imply that the content of certain parts of that book has been *totally misunderstood*.

Now, one would think an observation with such profound implications ought to be regarded as a brilliant contribution to critical scholarship. It deserves a Nobel prize, or whatever the equivalent of that is in critical scholarship. However, I am not holding my breath. Nor am I going to try submitting articles on this to journals. Those observations are so obvious to anyone in the know that if they had any chance of a favourable peer review they would already be out there. So why aren't they?

To put it bluntly, the reason is probably that mainstream scholars are *scared* of drawing attention to them. To do so could ruin their careers. It would mean going against a scholarly tradition that is now a couple of centuries old and widely regarded as the enlightened consensus. You see, what those observations imply is that certain passages in the book of Daniel were actually intended to be interpreted as *predictions of the distant future* – a view that would make anyone who holds it seem sympathetic to the claims of conservative (religious) interpreters of Daniel. Since the faith-based approach of those so-called 'conservative scholars' is considered unscientific and unenlightened by mainstream scholars (rightly in my opinion), this would render such a person vulnerable to career-damaging criticism from peers who will be eager to demonstrate their own commitment to the "enlightened" tradition.

Of course, the book of Daniel does *say* that it predicts the distant future. However, the current scholarly consensus is that, with one notable exception, all its prophecies of nonreligious events were intended to predict only events that had *already taken place* at the time it was written. In other words, critical scholars currently date the whole book much later than it claims, and insist that all its non-religious predictions *bar one* were meant to be interpreted as *past* events by its readers (a claim that this book calls into question).

The one exception is Daniel 11:40-45 (p.123) – a predicted *third* conquest of Egypt by that Seleucid king of Syria portrayed earlier. Many think this passage was the writer *genuinely predicting the future*. The reason they think so is because it appears to be totally wrong about certain details a writer living shortly after the time it seems to be referring to would be unlikely not to know about. The view that *this* passage is a *genuine prediction* appeals to critical scholars, not only because of its inaccuracy, but also because they are well aware that any writer hoping to pass off the book of Daniel as 'the recently discovered work of an ancient prophet' would be seriously worried that skeptics would simply denounce it as a forgery. One argument those skeptics were likely to make is that all the nonreligious events it predicted had already taken place. By inserting Daniel 11:40-45 – **a prediction that makes the last prophecy in the book extend *beyond the time of the book's publication*** (which, for reasons given in chapter 2, was around 165 BC) – the writer was probably providing himself and gullible readers with evidence designed to refute that anticipated denounce-ment, and perhaps even a reason to hold onto the book: The desire to see if what was yet to happen would actually come about.

You might now be wondering what could possibly be so bad about suggesting – as I hinted at earlier – that some *other* passage in the book of Daniel was similarly included to provide a prediction of the future for the same purpose. If so, you have an extremely good point. It would clearly have been in the interests of the proposed writer to include *more* such predictions to confuse the skeptical reader. Any passage predicting nonreligious events that is likely to have been interpreted as a prediction of the future by the intended readers of this book was therefore probably included *for this very purpose.* So does the book of Daniel contain other such passages?

Critical scholars say no. But for the reasons I have just mentioned, it is in their interests to deny this possibility. If they didn't, they could be labelled 'conservative' (i.e. 'religious'), which would not be good for their career in critical scholarship. The observations I will tell you about shortly indicate that the true answer is yes. There are in fact *three* more passages besides Daniel 11:40-45 that appear to have been intended as real predictions: Daniel 2:31-45, 7:1-27 and 9:24-27. And like that accepted prediction, those other examples of apparent 'guesswork' specify events of major historical significance that anyone living shortly after them would be expected to know about. The problem for mainstream scholars – and the really fascinating thing for the rest of us – is that, unlike Daniel 11:40-45, the events predicted by those other examples of genuine prediction *all came true exactly as the passage specifies*.

Ironically, this fact isn't widely appreciated even by conservative (religious) scholars of Daniel. Owing to a bias against appearing too critical of scripture and traditional Christian theology, those scholars have largely failed to notice just how amazingly well these passages portray established history. That's because to see this, one has to interpret each prophecy the way its *intended readers* would have interpreted it, and conservative (religious) scholars are decidedly reluctant to acknowledge that those intended readers were most probably living around 165 BC, *more than three centuries after Daniel is said to have received these prophecies.*

Now, you might be thinking that even if the book of Daniel was put together at that late date these prophecies could still have been originally penned by the prophet Daniel himself way back in the sixth century BC – especially if they predict events beyond 165 BC with supernatural accuracy as I am claiming. This again is a very good point. If the writer of the book of Daniel in the second century BC wanted to include specific predictions of the future that stood any chance of proving accurate, he was very likely to choose the words of a prophet whose predictions had *already proven reliable* (and therefore somebody who lived long enough ago for the accuracy of his predictions to be evident from hindsight).

Nevertheless, that does not change who we should regard to be the intended readers of these prophecies. Due to the fact that the writer responsible for the final form of the book of Daniel could have *changed the wording or context* of any part of those prophecies, it is what *he* meant by them that counts. We cannot know for certain whether or not he has accurately re-presented the original meaning of those passages. Consequently, the best we can do is to determine what *he* intended them to mean. To find out what that is most likely to be, we must therefore see how *his* intended readers – the Jews of *his day* – were most likely to interpret those passages. It's also worth remembering that these prophecies might not have meant anything *at all* to that writer. He might merely have been collecting together some ancient, prophecy-like texts. Hence, what his *intended readers* would have made of them is all-important.

As you can see from Daniel 12:1-4 below, this writer and his intended readers were living at a time that he refers to as 'the time of the end'. Although often taken to mean 'the end of the world', the actual meaning of this 'end' is left ambiguous. It may have meant the end of Israel as a nation, or the end of the sufferings of her people; or even the end of a king who was oppressing the Jewish people (as in Daniel 9:27 – see p.18). So my claim that the writer has included prophecies predicting events *beyond* this 'end time' is not in the least bit ruled out by this term. And in any case, since this passage predicts everlasting life for some, there is clearly plenty of time after this End for future events to unfold. It says:

> **Dan 12:1-4** [1]...there will be a time of trouble such as never was since there was a nation up to that same time. At that time your people will be delivered, everyone who is found written in the book. [2]Many of those who sleep in the dust of the earth will awake, some to everlasting life, and some to shame and everlasting contempt. [3]Those who are wise will shine as the brightness of the expanse. Those who turn many to righteousness will shine as the stars forever and ever. [4]But you, Daniel, **shut up the words, and seal the book, even to the time of the end**.

Notice how the final command here "explains" why those readers are the first to see this prophecy. Let us now consider the *more likely* reason, and establish the identity of those intended readers.

Now I will show you the truth.
Behold, three more kings will arise in Persia;
and the fourth will be far richer than all of them.
When he has grown strong through his riches,
he will stir up all against the realm of Greece.
A mighty king will arise, who will rule with great dominion,
and do according to his will.
When he has arisen, his kingdom will be broken,
and will be divided toward the four winds of heaven,
but not to his posterity,
nor according to his dominion with which he ruled;
for his kingdom will be plucked up, even for others besides these.
The king of the south will be strong.
One of his princes will become stronger than him,
and have dominion.
His dominion will be a great dominion.

Daniel 11:2-5 (The Rise of the Seleucid Empire)

You shall sow your field for six years,
and you shall prune your vineyard for six years, and gather in its fruits;
but in the seventh year there shall be a Sabbath
of solemn rest for the land, a Sabbath to Yahweh.
You shall not sow your field or prune your vineyard.

Leviticus 25:3-4 (The Weeks of Seven Years in Jewish Law)

2. How the Intended Readers Perceived their History

Conveniently, the book of Daniel itself gives us a fairly good idea of who its intended readers were, and how they perceived their recent history. It is almost as if it were *designed* to do this. The bit of unfulfilled guesswork that I mentioned earlier (Daniel 11:40-45) is pinned onto the end of a detailed sequence of historical events (Daniel 11:2-39). This allows one to date the writing of Daniel 11 quite precisely to between 167 BC (the time of its last *accurate* reference) and 164 BC (the year its guesswork *failed to come true*). And since it introduces Daniel 12 and appears to borrow certain words from other parts of Daniel (such as the 'abomination' phrase mentioned in my Preface), we can be fairly confident that the book itself was completed around that time. Remember, in this book we are only interested in what a scientific person who makes no religious assumptions ought to conclude – i.e. the most *rational* view.

The main focus of Daniel 11-12 (see p.123) is the attacks upon the Jewish faith that I illustrated in chapter 1. The work of a Greek (Seleucid) king called Antiochus Epiphanes, these were ongoing when most think this passage was written. In view of this, the fact that it exhorts the Jews to stand firm in the face of such hardship, promising everlasting life (Dan 12:2, p.9) for those who do, means it was very likely designed to *inspire* such resilience in the faithful.

Hence the mainstream conclusion that this was the purpose of the book of Daniel is a sound one. Its intended readers were therefore almost certainly the persecuted Jews of Judea, suffering under Epiphanes around 165 BC. And their perception of history, as far as we can tell, will thus be that which is evident in Daniel 11:2-39, the relatively accurate part of the long prophecy in Daniel 11-12.

However, that is not the only evidence of that early Jewish perception of history that the compiler of the book of Daniel (the 165 BC writer) has left us with. Amazingly, he has also included another prophecy that covers exactly the same ground as Daniel 11-12 but in the form of *dream imagery with accompanying interpretation*. That prophecy is Daniel 8 (p.121), and its inclusion is extremely convenient for us because two of the passages that I am claiming to be real predictions (Daniel 7 and Daniel 2:31-45) have exactly this format. The fact that the compiler has already translated his perception of history into this format shows that he is not leaving his readers to interpret those intriguing passages any way they like. He is making *his* interpretation of them *as clear as he can* without completely ruining the illusion that the book of Daniel is a work of ancient prophecy as opposed to recent commentary.

But in doing so, he has shown us exactly what *we* ought to think of these passages. For reasons that will be crystallised in chapters 8-10, what he says in Daniel 8 makes it abundantly clear that he intended Daniel 7 and Daniel 2 to be understood as *predictions of the distant future*. Their purpose was to persuade skeptical readers to withhold their denouncement of this book until time had shown whether or not these prophecies were accurate. Yet this is not what critical scholars currently make of them. Critical scholars all argue that they were each merely a poor attempt at predicting the main events related in detail in Daniel 8 and Daniel 11. Their consequent redundancy is explained away with the claim that the writer felt that imperfect predictions of those same events were necessary to build up the illusion of a vision of the future gradually becoming clearer as the book of Daniel progresses. However, this is not the impression one gets from a careful reading.

The content of Daniel 7 and 2 (p. xv) is in fact *vastly different* from that of Daniel 8 and 11. This fact is put down to them being written by a different person who had a very different perception of history from the writer of Daniel 11, and a fairly poor knowledge of current affairs. Yet, as you will see in chapters 8-10, this theory is not supported by the evidence found in Daniel 8 and Daniel 11 and elsewhere in the book of Daniel. That evidence strongly supports my claim that the compiler included Daniel 7 and 2 for essentially the same reason he included Daniel 11:40-45. They were intended to be understood as predictions that extend into the distant future, and which bear no mention of the current persecution. They were inserted to create the illusion that the book of Daniel was not the fake propaganda designed to inspire resilience in the face of the present hardships that skeptics were likely to suggest. It was really an authentic biographical work containing genuine prophecies that predicted the current crisis *but by no means exclusively*. Yet this obvious possibility appears not to have crossed the minds of the many people who have commented upon the book of Daniel. From the evidence I list in chapters 8-10, I find this quite remarkable.

Of course, right now you are probably wondering if I have really got it right. If no distinguished scholar supports this position surely there has to be something wrong with it. If that is you, have a look at the observations in this book that other scholars appear to have missed – in particular chapters 4, 5, 8, 9 and 17 – and ask yourself if you ought to trust any view of the book of Daniel that does not take these facts into account. As I said before, the reason scholars avoid the position I am advocating is quite understandable. When these observations are taken into account, the prophecies in question can only be reasonably interpreted as *intentional predictions of the future* far beyond the time they were included in the book of Daniel. And when you examine the history of the times they refer to, they appear to have come true to a rather astonishing extent. If critical scholars were to interpret them in the way most justified by the content of Daniel, they would be forced to admit that these prophecies *do in fact appear to be both genuine and accurate*, which is precisely what many religious scholars claim about them. Moreover, the events that appear to have fulfilled them were pivotal moments in the rise of Christianity. Critical scholars have no wish to appear in favour of such claims. As a result, they stick rigidly to the established 'consensus' regardless of its inconsistencies – a consensus formed by other critical scholars faced with exactly the same dilemma – and they avoid any mention of that *far more satisfactory* alternative explanation. They don't even debate its merits. If they did, they'd be forced to admit that it is a lot more convincing than the account they currently adhere to – and it isn't rendered any less likely by the fact that history appears to have fulfilled the passages it identifies as 'guesswork'.

If a prediction could not have been written *from hindsight* – if it couldn't be what scholars call an *ex eventu* prophecy – whether or not it happens to have been fulfilled by subsequent events ought to be considered *completely irrelevant* as far as the debate over its intended purpose is concerned. Despite what religious interpreters of Daniel often claim, an accurate fulfilment of genuine prophecy doesn't automatically entail something unusual or supernatural. The prediction could have come true by pure chance, or by the deliberate efforts of individuals trying to *make* it come true. What is really interesting about the fulfilment of Daniel 7 and Daniel 2, and also Daniel 9 as we are about to discover, is that in these cases such 'rational' explanations *do not seem to be an option*.

We shall look first at Daniel 9. Before we do so, though, I should mention that the book of Daniel is bilingual. In its oldest extant manuscripts, Daniel 1 and Daniel 8-12 are in *Hebrew*, whereas apart from the first three-and-a-half verses of Daniel 2, Daniel 2-7 is in *Aramaic*. Hence, two of the three prophecies of interest were written in Aramaic. However, my proposal strongly implies that all three of these prophecies came from the same source – someone the compiler thought could see into the future. If true, that would mean they were probably all originally in Aramaic. In the current book, Daniel 9 happens to be in Hebrew, just like the *ex eventu* prophecies found in Daniel 8 and Daniel 11. But Daniel 9 consists mainly of a prayer that many scholars think was added *after* the very short prophecy at its end. If that prophecy had originally been written in Aramaic and the prayer in Hebrew, the compiler would have had good reason to translate the prophecy into Hebrew too. Hence its current language does not conflict with my hypothesis.

The analysis that follows will require a little bit of effort. So, to give you an idea of what you will discover if you persevere with the next five chapters consider this modern analogy. Imagine that back in 2009 you bought a large old house in a fictitious town called Jule. The house is known as *West Jule Manor* (an anagram), and along with the original title deeds you find a note that reads:

> *In the five thousand, seven hundred and ninety-sixth month after permission is given to build the Manor in the West of Jule a famous leader called Iona Dent will visit.*

Mysterious, isn't it! Noticing that the deeds are dated to late February 1534, you do the sum and find that it points to February 2017! Excited at the chance to see if this strange prediction comes true you decide to stay in that property for the next eight years, and you make sure you're not away that February. Nothing unexpected happens. You wait the full month. But there's no sign of Ms Dent. Disappointed, you confide in a friend who mentions that a singer who visited you a few years ago is now calling herself *Iona Dent* after hearing about your strange discovery. Several weeks later, you happen to hear on the radio that her song *West Jule Manor* has reached Number One. Reminded of the 'famous leader' part of the prophecy, you try to remember when exactly that singer visited.

Although the day eludes you, it must have been a few weeks before the Easter break in 2010 because you had promised her you would attend her next concert but were unable to do so due to air-traffic disruption caused by a volcano in Iceland. That makes it late March or early April. Intrigued, you look again at the prediction. It clearly says 5796 months. That's 2017, not 2010. You are about to dismiss your interest as just a silly obsession, but then you notice what seems an unlikely error: The deeds are dated *30th* February.

Fascinated by this, you enquire in the local library and discover why. At the start of 1534, the very year your house was built, a now-largely-forgotten religious group running the town of Jule attempted to introduce their own reform to the Julian calendar. They decided to make all the months *thirty days long*. Instead of introducing an extra day every four years as we do, they added an extra month every six years, (and planned to add a month every century as well, to make up the difference that our leap years fill).

On hearing this, a thought occurs to you: The months the writer of the prophecy was thinking of were all *thirty days long*. Not really expecting anything surprising, you quickly multiply the 5796 by 30 to find out how many days it is, and then divide by the number of days in a full solar year (365.2422) to get the number of years you will need to count forward from the date of your deeds (1st March 1534, which was *11th March* after the Gregorian reform of 1582). You then take the decimal fraction and times it by twelve to find out roughly how many extra months to add on. Very quickly you discover to your amazement that the visit of this singer where you had discussed the prophecy that inspired her to write the very song that had now made her famous *had indeed* definitely taken place within the 5796th 30-day month after the date on your title deeds!

Would you be utterly astonished by such a coincidence? If so, you will be mesmerised by the accuracy of the prophecy we shall now examine. Its fulfilment (chapters 6 & 7) was even *more* surprising.

3. The Seventy 'Sevens' Prophecy in Daniel 9

Daniel 9:24-27 is perhaps the most famous of Daniel's prophecies. Renowned scientist Sir Isaac Newton described it as *the foundation of Christianity*, and it has certainly been used by many Christians as justification for their faith. That is because it specifies a time interval that ends with a 'Christ' (or 'Anointed One' – the Hebrew word is 'Messiah') who would be *a ruler or king*, and *get executed*. Moreover, since the prophecy is about Daniel's 'holy city' of Jerusalem, one can justifiably conclude that this end-point is a notable *arrival* of this Christ *at Jerusalem*. It says the following:

> **Dan 9:24-27** 24Seventy "sevens" are determined for your people and your holy city to finish disobedience, to make an end of sin, to atone for iniquity, to bring in everlasting righteousness, to seal up vision and prophecy, and **to anoint the Most Holy.**
>
> 25Know and understand this: **From the going out of the word to restore and rebuild Jerusalem until an <u>Anointed One</u> [a 'Christ'], a *ruler* [as in 'an *exalted leader or king*'], there will be seven "sevens", and sixty-two "sevens"** [i.e. 69 "sevens"]. **It will be built again with streets and a trench** [or 'moat' – i.e. surrounding defences], **but in times of trouble.**

²⁶After the sixty-two "sevens", the <u>Anointed One</u> [the 'Christ'] will be put to death and will have nothing.

The people of *the ruler who will come* will destroy the city and the sanctuary. **His end** will be with a flood [the subject here could also be 'Its', but 'His' seems implied by verse 27]. War will go on until the end. Desolations have been determined.

²⁷He will confirm a covenant with many for one "seven". In the middle of the "seven" he will cause the sacrifice and offering to cease. And on an overspreading [or 'wing'] he will set up the abomination of desolation, even until **the full end, that which is determined, is poured out on him.** [Or: 'on the wing of abominations will come one who makes desolate, even until a full end, that which is determined, is poured out on him (or 'on it' (the desolate) which makes very little sense in this context).]

Almost all scholars agree that the 'sevens' here are the *weeks of seven years* in the Jewish law (Lev. 25:3-4, see p.10), and that this places the predicted 'Anointed One' (which is 'Christ' in Greek) *long after 165 BC when the book of Daniel was completed.* Sixty-nine 'sevens' after 539 BC, the year Daniel supposedly *received* this prophecy, brings one to the *50s* BC (and the starting point seems to be *later* than 539 BC). One of the puzzling features of the mainstream treatment of this passage is that critical scholars don't ever consider that this might have been the compiler's *intention*.

That's puzzling because, as I have already mentioned, a prophecy reaching far into the future of his own time was exactly what the writer of Daniel needed in order to ensure his work wasn't rejected as a forgery. It is true that certain events mentioned in verse 27 are reminiscent of events that had taken place in Jerusalem shortly before the 165 BC date of writing. Jewish sacrifice and offering had indeed been stopped at that time. It had been forcibly replaced with Greek sacrifice by a Seleucid (Greek) king called Antiochus Epiphanes. And what Jews would describe as an *abomination* (a foreign idol) had indeed been erected in their Temple, desolating it. But is this sufficient reason to assume that 'the ruler who will come' whose people will 'destroy the city and the sanctuary' is intended to be that Greek king *regardless of the impossibly long time period?* Is it not just about possible that the compiler of the book of Daniel would choose to insert a prophecy of events that bore some resemblance to those that were on his readers' minds precisely because it would make them examine this prophecy in detail and thereby work out that its time period was in fact *far too long?* They would thus discover that this was a prophecy about the future. It was not about those recent events at all, and so those skeptics who were claiming that it was, and doubting the authenticity of this book on that basis, were wrong. In that case, its parallels with the recent acts of Antiochus Epiphanes would merely be intended to draw the reader's *attention* to it.

As you will have guessed, critical scholars appear not to have considered this possibility. Yet, besides the length and derived appearance of the time period (which strongly supports this view), there's a surprising amount of evidence in its favour. For a start, prior to the erecting of the 'abomination', and the ending of sacrifice and offering, the prophecy predicts the *destruction of the Jerusalem Temple* (the sanctuary, v.26) which Epiphanes' soldiers plundered **but did not destroy**. Moreover, it seems to predict that Jerusalem would be destroyed *a long time* (several years at least) before the ending of sacrifice and offering. Epiphanes' soldiers did destroy parts of Jerusalem, but only *weeks* before they established pagan sacrifices in place of Jewish ones at the Jerusalem Temple.

An argument that could be made against this proposal is the fact that the phrase 'abomination of desolation' found in some trans-lations of Daniel 9 is used in Daniel 11:31 (p.123) to refer to the idol that Epiphanes had erected. That, however, is also what we should expect if the author wants the predicted events in Daniel 9 to appear somewhat similar to those of Daniel 11. The fact that this phrase is used in Daniel 9 does not by any means suggest that the author thinks the abomination mentioned in that prophecy is the same one he is referring to in Daniel 11. The only thing that would suggest *this* is if the *time period* can be reconciled with this claim. The fact that there is no hint of such a time period in the detailed prophecies of Daniel 11 and Daniel 8 immediately suggests that either it cannot, or the writer did not intend it to be. Nevertheless, this has not stopped critical scholars going to great pains to try to work out a way in which this might be done. Perhaps, they speculate, the writer was thinking of a 'word to restore and rebuild Jerusalem' (v.25, p.17) that was issued *long before* the time Daniel supposedly received this prophecy; or perhaps he didn't really have any idea how much time had passed and was just choosing that symbolic-sounding round number to link this prophecy with a 'seventy years' prophecy of Jeremiah's mentioned in Daniel 9:2.

As you will now see, there is robust evidence against *both* these proposals. And that evidence seems to me to have been covered up by critical scholars. **It is the stunning resemblance of the prayer in Daniel 9 to a prayer found in** *Nehemiah 1* – a prayer prayed by Jerusalem's famous wall-builder Nehemiah, and prompted, just like Daniel's, by the dilapidated state of that 'holy city' (which still lay in ruins when this prayer was prayed, almost a hundred years after Daniel reportedly received his prophecy of its rebuilding).

This resemblance is of paramount significance because it was in answer to that very prayer in 444 BC that Nehemiah was granted his *royal permission to rebuild Jerusalem* – an event recorded in Nehemiah 2:1-8 (p.23). As far as I can see, this completely settles the question of what the compiler of the book of Daniel thought the '**word to restore and rebuild Jerusalem**' in Daniel 9:25 was. If he based the prayer in Daniel 9 on that of Nehemiah 1, as this resemblance suggests, he was obviously thinking of Nehemiah's permission to restore and rebuild Jerusalem as the starting point of the time period that the prophecy contains. If he hadn't been, he would still have had that permission on his mind, and one would therefore expect this passage to give some indication that this was *not* the intended starting point. The fact that there is no such indication strongly supports the view that Nehemiah's permission *was* the intended starting point. It is worth noting that there's no other known decree that specifically permits the Jews to rebuild Jerusalem (see * p.22). The intended readers of the book of Daniel were bound to *think* this was the one. So the absence of any contrary indication suggests that this was indeed what the writer of Daniel 9 *intended* them to think. It is therefore quite amazing no critical scholar favours this view. I find it hard to believe they aren't *aware* of the resemblance of Daniel 9 to Nehemiah 1.

In fact, the occasional mainstream scholar does mention this resemblance in passing. For instance, **Knight 1971 (p.447) cites this prayer and another in the book of Nehemiah as his *only* examples of language similar to Daniel 9:4-19**. Collins 1984 (p.92) makes it one of seven with similar *structure* to Daniel 9. However, these scholars don't examine that likeness in any detail. Nor do they point out how similar the *context* of that first prayer in the book of Nehemiah is to that of Daniel's prayer. They don't inform their readers that this prayer of Nehemiah's was a response to the desolate state of Jerusalem, *just like Daniel's is*. And they never point out that it was prayed after a period of mourning and fasting, *exactly as we find in Daniel 9*. Incredibly, they don't even mention that it was followed by *a royal permission to rebuild Jerusalem*, just as Daniel's prayer is answered by a *prophecy* of Jerusalem's rebuilding that refers to *just such a royal permission*.

These observations seem to me to be far from trivial. Critical scholars frequently propose dependences between texts that have a lot *less* in common. So it really surprises me that they don't do the same for Daniel 9 and Nehemiah 1. They are perhaps trying to suggest that Daniel's prayer may have been *written around the same time as* Nehemiah's, rather than being *derived from it at a later date*. That is because, if the latter were the case, the most likely candidate for the author of that prayer would be the compiler of the book of Daniel, making it totally unreasonable to argue that he did not intend his 'word to restore and rebuild Jerusalem' to be the one given to Nehemiah. But since that prayer serves so well as a dramatic introduction to the prophecy that follows it, shouldn't scholars *expect* it to have been constructed for this purpose?

As you will see in the next chapter, the frequent repetition in Daniel 9, and its striking similarities to Nehemiah 1, strongly favour this view. It is perhaps for this reason that critical scholars don't highlight these similarities. They have no wish to promote the idea that Daniel's 'word to restore and rebuild Jerusalem' was Nehemiah's famous permission because that is precisely the view of many conservative scholars. It makes the prophecy perfectly fulfilled *by Christ*. We shall now go against the wishes of those mainstream scholars and examine that hidden evidence in some detail.

NOTES RELATING TO CHAPTER 3

* Three other royal decrees have been proposed (Ezra 1:1-4, Ezra 6:1-12, and Ezra 7:12-26), together with certain Old Testament prophecies (Jeremiah 25:11, 29:10, 30:18, Isaiah 44:28, and even Daniel 9:24-27 itself). However, other than Daniel 9 itself, the proposed prophecies all precede the issuing of Daniel 9. This means they can be dismissed on the grounds that if Daniel were supposed to know about 'the word to restore and rebuild Jerusalem', Daniel 9 would be expected to say 'as spoken of by [name of prophet]'. The fact that no such information is given thus favours the view that a 'future' decree was intended. If it were meant instead to be Daniel 9 itself, one would expect the prophecy to say '*this* word...' where it actually says '*the* word...'. A second reason to doubt that the writer was referring to any of these prophecies is that, if it were meant to be a prophecy, one would expect Daniel 9 to say '*my* word' or 'the word *of the Lord*'. Again, it does not. And a third reason is that none of the proposed prophecies are *easily dated to a particular year*. This makes them quite unsuitable for serving the purpose the writer clearly intends his 'word to restore

and rebuild Jerusalem' to serve. Although the other *royal decrees* that have been proposed do come after the date of Daniel 9, and *are* clearly dated, none of them permits the rebuilding of *the city and its defences*, which is what Daniel 9:25 really emphasises (see p.17). Had a word to rebuild the Temple been intended, one would expect Daniel 9:25 to say 'the sanctuary' rather than 'Jerusalem'.

By far the most popular of those temple restoration decrees is the Edict of Cyrus given in Ezra 1:1-4, below:

> **Ezra 1:1-4** [1]Now in the first year of Cyrus king of Persia, that Yahweh's word by Jeremiah's mouth might be accomplished, Yahweh stirred up the spirit of Cyrus king of Persia, so that he made a proclamation throughout all his kingdom, and put it also in writing, saying, [2]"Thus says Cyrus king of Persia, 'Yahweh, the God of heaven, has given me all the kingdoms of the earth; and he has commanded me to build him a house in Jerusalem, which is in Judah. [3]Whoever there is among you of all his people, may his God be with him, and let him go up to Jerusalem, which is in Judah, and build the house of Yahweh, the God of Israel (he is God), which is in Jerusalem. [4]Whoever is left, in any place where he lives, let the men of his place help him with silver, with gold, with goods, and with animals, in addition to the freewill offering for God's house which is in Jerusalem.'"

As you can see, this royal decree, which is by far the best of the three alternatives to Nehemiah's permission, only permits the restoration of the Temple ('the sanctuary' of Daniel 9). That is why Jerusalem was still in a state of disrepair when Nehemiah enquired about it almost a century later 'in the month of Chislev, in the twentieth year [of Artaxerxes]' (Neh 1:1). Compare this 'Edict of Cyrus' with the permission given to Nehemiah shortly after he prayed the prayer that is so similar to Daniel's. You'll find it in Nehemiah 2:1-8, below:

> **Neh 2:1-8** [1]In the month Nisan, in the twentieth year of Artaxerxes the king, when wine was before him, I picked up the wine, and gave it to the king. Now I had not been sad before in his presence. [2]The king said to me, "Why is your face sad, since you are not sick? This is nothing else but sorrow of heart." Then I was very much afraid. [3]I said to the king, "Let the king live

forever! Why shouldn't my face be sad, when the city, the place of my fathers' tombs, lies waste, and its gates have been consumed with fire?"

⁴Then the king said to me, "What is your request?"

So I prayed to the God of heaven. ⁵I said to the king, "If it pleases the king, and if your servant has found favour in your sight, that you would send me to Judah, to the city of my fathers' tombs, **that I may build it**."

⁶The king said to me (the queen was also sitting by him), "How long will your journey be? When will you return?"

So it pleased the king to send me, and I set a time for him. ⁷Moreover I said to the king, "If it pleases the king, let letters be given me to the governors beyond the River, that they may let me pass through until I come to Judah; ⁸and a letter to Asaph the keeper of the king's forest, that he may give me timber to make beams for the gates of the citadel by the temple, for the wall of the city, and for the house that I will occupy."

The king granted my requests, because of the good hand of my God on me.

Unlike the Edict of Cyrus, this royal permission (the letters Nehemiah received from king Artaxerxes I of Persia) *clearly permits the Jews to rebuild Jerusalem.* Since this passage would have been well known at the time the book of Daniel was written, and since Nehemiah, unlike Cyrus, was a famous *Jewish* leader, don't you think the intended readers of the book of Daniel would be more likely to think that *this* royal permission was what the prophecy in Daniel 9 was referring to? Considering that Daniel 9 makes no attempt to exclude this most obvious interpretation, and in view of the fact that verse 25 (p.17) actually *encourages* it with its emphasis on the rebuilding of the city and its defences, I suspect that this is exactly what the compiler *intended* them to think. As you will see in the next chapter, the prayer that introduces this prophecy was probably derived from the very prayer to which Nehemiah *attributes* his permission to rebuild Jerusalem. For me, this is conclusive evidence. If the compiler of Daniel 9 inserted a prayer derived from the one that resulted in Nehemiah's word to restore and rebuild Jerusalem, that simply *must* be what he meant by the 'word to restore and rebuild Jerusalem' in Daniel 9. That should not be in doubt.

4. The Similarity of Daniel 9 to Nehemiah 1

Was the prayer in Daniel 9 based on Nehemiah 1:5-11? Let's look at the evidence: After recording the date, and telling us how he was reminded of the desolate state of Jerusalem, and how he mourned and fasted as a result, Nehemiah begins his prayer as follows:

> NEH 1: ⁵I beg you, **Yahweh**, the God of heaven, **the great and awesome God, who keeps his covenant of love with those who love him and keep his commandments...**

Following a similar intro, including the tears and fasting, Daniel's prayer (Daniel 9:4-19) starts with almost exactly the same words:

> DAN 9: ⁴I prayed to **Yahweh** my God, and made confession, and said, "Oh lord, **the great and awesome God, who keeps his covenant of love with those who love him and keep his commandments...**

After a verse appealing to God to **open his eyes and ears** so he can hear the prayer his servant is praying at this time, day and night, for the children of Israel whose sins he is confessing, which sounds rather like Daniel 9:18 ('**My God, turn your ear, and hear. Open your eyes and see...**'), Nehemiah goes on to confess:

NEH 1: [we] have sinned. ⁷We have dealt very corruptly against you. We have not obeyed the commands, nor the decrees, nor the laws that you gave your servant Moses.

The very next couple of verses of *Daniel's* prayer says pretty much the same thing, with 'the prophets' in place of 'Moses':

DAN 9: ⁵we have sinned, and have dealt corruptly, and have done wickedly, and have rebelled, even turning aside from your commands and from your laws. ⁶We have not listened to your servants the prophets, who spoke in your name to our kings, our princes and our ancestors, and to all the people of the land.

The fourth verse of Nehemiah's prayer then reminds God of an instruction he gave to Moses (the most famous of those prophets):

NEH 1: ⁸Remember, I beg you, the instruction you gave your servant Moses, saying, 'If you are unfaithful, I will scatter you among the peoples;

Astonishingly, in the fourth verse of Daniel's prayer we find what appears to be an acknowledgement of the fulfilment of that very same instruction (How likely is that to be just chance?):

DAN 9: ⁷Lord, righteousness belongs to you, but to us shame, as it is today—to the men of Judah, and the inhabitants of Jerusalem, and to all Israel, both near and far off, in all the countries where you have scattered us, because of our unfaithfulness to you.

The fact that this prayer not only refers to the same Mosaic instruction as Nehemiah's but does so *at roughly the same place* is very strong evidence of dependence. And more follows. The next verse of Nehemiah 1 focusses on God's mercy and forgiveness:

<u>NEH 1</u>: [9]but if you return to me, and keep my commandments and do them, though your outcasts were in the uttermost part of the heavens, **yet I will gather them from there, and will bring them to the place that I have chosen, to cause my name to dwell there.**

And likewise, so does the next couple of verses of *Daniel 9*:

<u>DAN 9</u>: [8]Lord, to us belongs shame, to our kings, to our princes, and to our fathers, because we have sinned against you. [9]**To the Lord our God belong mercies and forgiveness**; even though we have rebelled against him.

The next five verses of Daniel's prayer appear to be an amplification of those previous two points: the extent to which the Israelites had been unfaithful to God, and the extent to which God's instruction to Moses had been fulfilled. This time the fulfilment is the desolation of Jerusalem rather than the scattering of her people. But notice how its justification is now the fulfilment of a Mosaic instruction, just as it is in *Nehemiah's* prayer:

<u>DAN 9</u>: [10]We haven't obeyed our God Yahweh's voice, to walk in his laws, which he set before us by his servants the prophets. [11]Yes, all Israel have transgressed your law, turning aside, that they should not obey your voice. Therefore, **the curse and the oath written in the law of Moses the servant of God has been poured out on us**; for we have sinned against him. [12]He has confirmed his words, which he spoke against us, and against our judges who judged us, by bringing on us a great evil; for under the whole heaven, nothing has been done like what has been done to Jerusalem. [13]**As it is written in the law of Moses, all this evil has come on us. Yet we have not entreated the favour of Yahweh our God**, that we should turn from our iniquities and have discernment in your truth. [14]Therefore **Yahweh has watched over the evil, and brought**

it on us; for Yahweh our God is righteous in all the things he does, and we have not obeyed his voice.

Interestingly, the last verse of this bit of amplification in Daniel 9 is extremely like verse 33 of Nehemiah *9* – a later prayer that the book of Nehemiah contains: That verse says,

NEH 9: **you** [O Yahweh our God] **are just in all that has come on us; for you have dealt truly, but we have done wickedly.**

Okay, it isn't identical. God is 'just' rather than 'righteous' in everything he does, and in spite of that, the Israelites have 'done wickedly' rather than 'not obeyed his voice'. But the meaning being expressed is identical, and the structure very similar. And as we shall see shortly, that verse is not the only connection between Daniel 9 and Nehemiah 9. It's almost as if Nehemiah 9 is being used as a source of further inspiration when the much shorter but far more relevant prayer of Nehemiah 1 is lacking.

But let's get back to our comparison of Daniel 9 with Nehemiah 1.

The next verse of Daniel 9 invokes Israel's redemption (the miraculous exodus of her people from slavery in Egypt), saying,

DAN 9: [15]Now, Lord our God, **who brought your people out of the land of Egypt with a mighty hand**, and **gained a name for yourself, as it is today**; we have sinned. We have done wickedly.

Almost predictably, the next verse of Nehemiah 1 *also* talks about this redemption in terms of God's 'mighty hand':

NEH 1: [10]Now these are your servants and your people, **whom you have redeemed** by your great power, and **by your mighty hand.**

Even more interestingly, this redemption is described specifically as *the Exodus from Egypt* in Nehemiah 9:10, where we also find the phrase '**and made a name for yourself as it is today**'. This to me seems clear evidence that Daniel 9 is closely based on both Nehemiah 1 and Nehemiah 9, with the latter being used merely to embellish the content found in Nehemiah 1 where appropriate. Although the next verse of Daniel 9 has no direct similarities with the text of Nehemiah, the 'righteous acts' it speaks of are almost certainly going to be those listed in detail in Nehemiah 9:27-31, and its 'object of scorn' phrase neatly sums up the sentiment of Nehemiah 9:36-37 (see Appendix p.126). Daniel 9:16 says,

> DAN 9: [16]Lord, in keeping with **all your righteous acts**, please let your anger and your wrath be turned away from your city of Jerusalem, your holy mountain. Because for our sins, and for the iniquities of our fathers, Jerusalem and your people have become an **object of scorn** to all who are around us.

Daniel 9 then begins its concluding petition:

> DAN 9: [17]Now therefore, our God, **listen to the prayer of your servant, and to his petitions**. For your sake, lord, cause your face to shine on your sanctuary that is desolate.

Notice how this is somewhat similar to the *conclusion* of Nehemiah 1:

> NEH 1: [11]Lord, I beg you, **let your ear be attentive now to the prayer of your servant, and to the prayer of your servants,** who delight to fear your name; and please prosper your servant today, and grant him compassion in the sight of this man.

The more-specific aim of Nehemiah's prayer (the success of his request to be allowed to rebuild Jerusalem) accounts for the differences here. But interestingly, Daniel's prayer isn't actually finished. It then goes on to pretty much summarise what has been said before, and that summary clearly reflects the structure and themes of Nehemiah 1, as you can see below:

> DAN 9: [18]My God, **turn your ear, and hear. Open your eyes, and see [Nehemiah 1:6]** our desolations, and **the city which is called by your name [Nehemiah 1:9]**; for we do not present our petitions before you because of our righteousness, but **for the sake of your great mercy [the theme of Nehemiah 1:9]**. [19]Lord, listen! Lord, forgive! Lord, hear and act! Don't defer, for your own sake, my God, since **your city and your people are called by your name**.

As we have seen, not only does the writer of Daniel 9 make his prayer emphasize the fact that Jerusalem is *the place of God's name* (the very definition found in Nehemiah 1), but he also begins his prayer with *the same words* as Nehemiah 1, includes a very similar *confession of national guilt*, makes its fourth verse respond to *the very same Mosaic instruction* that Nehemiah refers to in the fourth verse of his prayer in Nehemiah 1, and mentions the redemption of Israel *by God's 'mighty hand'* in the build-up to his concluding petition, exactly like Nehemiah 1. Both prayers also use the same name for God (a name not used elsewhere in the book of Daniel), and implore him to *open his eyes and ears*.

I think this is very clear evidence that the writer of Daniel's prayer was deriving it from that first prayer in the book of Nehemiah. This is certainly possible because the book of Daniel was put together around 165 BC, almost 280 years *after* Nehemiah prayed the prayer he has recorded in his memoir (which is widely thought to be original and thus dates from when it claims – 444 BC or a bit later in Nehemiah's life). The slight chance that Daniel's prayer existed as a separate work that inspired Nehemiah seems to me to be ruled out by the brevity of Nehemiah's prayer compared to Daniel's. The latter clearly grew out of the former, not vice versa.

It's worth noting that some scholars *do* hint that the inspiration for Daniel's prayer might have come from the book of Nehemiah (see e.g. Barton 2002, p.663). The puzzling thing is that these scholars emphasize *Nehemiah 9* as the possible inspiration for Daniel 9. They make no mention of Nehemiah 1, even though that first prayer in the book of Nehemiah has *far more* in common with Daniel 9 than the later one does. What could possibly be the reason for this omission? Have those expert scholars really failed to notice this resemblance? I don't think so. We're talking about *expert scholars*, here, not the average reader. And besides, as we saw in chapter 3 (p.21), some mainstream scholars *have* mentioned it in passing. Knight's *only* Daniel-9-like comparisons were Nehemiah 1 and 9. Hence, either those others all just happen to be *forgetting* about it when writing their detailed analyses, or what it implies for the critical consensus on Daniel 9 is *putting them off* discussing it.

The problem is that the prayer in Nehemiah 1 comes just before Nehemiah's account of how he received his permission to restore and rebuild Jerusalem (see Nehemiah 2:1-8, p.23-24). Were critical scholars to acknowledge the dependence of Daniel 9 on Nehemiah 1, someone was bound to point out that this surely means **the writer of Daniel 9 intended 'the word to restore and rebuild Jerusalem' in the prophecy of that chapter to be Nehemiah's permission**. Why else would he have based Daniel's prayer on Nehemiah 1? After all, he could have just made it up himself, or based it on some other Old Testament prayer. At the very least, the fact that he drew inspiration from Nehemiah 1 means that he would have had Nehemiah's permission (Nehemiah 2:1-8) *on his mind* when inserting the 'Seventy 'sevens'' prophecy into this chapter. Hence the fact that there is no attempt to exclude this very obvious possibility pretty much guarantees that this is 'the word to restore and rebuild Jerusalem' that the writer was thinking of.

But why don't critical scholars just accept this? Why do they continually try to argue that it was some other decree? It is true that this permission was granted to Nehemiah only around *280 years* (40 'sevens') prior to the completion of the book of Daniel, rather than the two-centuries-longer *483 years* (69 'sevens') that an accurate fulfilment of the mainstream interpretation of this prophecy would require. (Remember, mainstream scholars assume that it was purely about events that had happened *before* the book of Daniel was completed). But mainstream scholars have never insisted that this prophecy is accurate. Couldn't they just claim that the writer wasn't too sure how much time had passed from the date of Nehemiah's permission? That date is given in Nehemiah 2:1 as 'the month of Nisan in the twentieth year of Artaxerxes'. If the writer of Daniel 9 had an incomplete record of the reign-lengths of the Persian emperors that followed Artaxerxes I (or the Greek kings that followed them), as is very likely, couldn't he simply have *overestimated* the time that had passed since then?

The reason critical scholars never endorse the view that this 'word to restore and rebuild Jerusalem' was Nehemiah's permission is because the answer to this question is *No!* The reason he would not have overestimated this time period is because he would not calculate it by adding up those reign-lengths. If he wanted to know how much time had passed since Nehemiah received his permission to restore and rebuild Jerusalem, all he had to do was ascertain how old the *walls* of Jerusalem were. After all, Nehemiah completed these walls in the same year he received his permission to build them (444 BC). As their completion was a pivotal moment in Jerusalem's restoration, it is very likely that anniversaries of it would have been celebrated every year since. But even if that were not the case, the fact that the residents of the city relied upon them for protection would make their age a regular topic of discussion that would easily preserve its memory. It's also worth noting that Nehemiah 3 meticulously lists all the people who took part in that building project along with the sections of wall that they rebuilt. Those sections of wall would have been a visible source of great pride for subsequent generations of their descendants, making it inconceivable that no resident of Jerusalem in 165 BC had any idea how old its walls were. Since the writer of the book of Daniel probably lived in or near Jerusalem, all he needed to do was pop down to his local and ask the older residents of the city.

But why should this fact stop critical scholars accepting that the 'word to restore and rebuild Jerusalem' in the prophecy was Nehemiah's permission? It's true that it means the prophecy could not be – and was never *meant* to be – about the recent actions of the Greek (Seleucid) king Antiochus Epiphanes that are described in Daniel 8 and Daniel 11 (see Appendix p.122-123). But as I said earlier, there is actually no good reason why it should be about those same events. The writer of Daniel had a strong motive to include passages predicting similar events to happen long *after* his own day: The need to protect his book from dismissal by skeptics. The similarities would get his readers interested in these passages, and the time periods would give them grounds to claim that the latter half of the book of Daniel was not just prophecies of recent events (and therefore very likely to be a forgery). It also contained predictions of *the distant future*, and was consequently worth holding onto *despite* the suspicious nature of Daniel 8 and Daniel 11.

As far as I can see, there is only one reason this very likely possibility is never entertained by critical scholars. It is because certain conservative (religious) scholars have pointed out that, with very reasonable assumptions about the 'sevens' in the prophetic time period, it makes the prophecy predict the arrival of an *'Anointed One'*, an *'exalted leader or king'* who would get put to death empty-handed (or 'having nothing' – see * p.34), on the *very month* (some say the very *day*) on which Jesus of Nazareth was triumphantly proclaimed 'King' at Jerusalem before being rejected and crucified a few days later. And Jesus has subsequently become known throughout the world as 'Christ', which is Greek for 'Anointed One'. In other words, critical scholars are nervous that if they point out that this passage is very likely to be a genuine prediction of the future, they are going to end up being labelled 'conservative'. The polarised nature of academic views on the book of Daniel is thus preventing those experts from investigating what appears to be by far the most *justifiable* explanation for the content of Daniel 9. And more seriously, it is thereby preventing the trusting secular reader from discovering the true improbability of a coincidence the nature of which has the potential to change, not only one's worldview, but one's whole attitude to life.

NOTES RELATING TO CHAPTER 4

* If the translation 'put to death' in Daniel 9:26 (p.18) is correct (the Hebrew literally means 'cut off'), then the phrase 'will have nothing', as many scholars have noted, doesn't make a great deal of sense. It could mean the Anointed One would have no worldly possessions at the time he gets put to death (he obviously won't have afterwards – unless of course he comes back to life!). It could also mean no descendants, or no one to help him (like the king in Daniel 11:45 – see Appendix p.124). But since we are not told anything to suggest that the Anointed One *ought* to have such things, this statement seems somewhat out of place. There is, however, one plausible solution to this mystery: Perhaps the writer of this prophecy intended his readers to identify the Anointed One, who is called the *Most Holy* in this passage (see next chapter), with the person referred to as the *Most High* in Daniel 7 (a vision we will begin to look at in chapter 8). Since this Most High person is probably represented by the 'one like a son of man' figure who gets enthroned in the same dream (see p.67), he is regarded as *the ruler of an everlasting world-wide kingdom*. The implication of Daniel 9:26 is that at the time he is put to death he will have none of that wealth and power.

Of course, for this explanation to work, this prophecy would need to have been positioned directly after Daniel 7 in an earlier version of the book. However, that is not too implausible. We have already seen how Daniel 8 and Daniel 10-12, and the prayer in Daniel 9, (all written in Hebrew) are likely to have been added to the Aramaic chapters (Daniel 2-7). If Daniel 9:24-27 were an epilogue to that Aramaic book, then it *would* come after Daniel 7. And a translation into Hebrew might explain why 'Most Holy' occurs instead of 'Most High'.

5. Why the Most Holy *is* the Anointed One

Another strange fact about critical commentaries on the book of Daniel is that they often claim the phrase 'Most Holy' in Daniel 9:24 (see p.17) refers to the *Jerusalem Temple Sanctuary*. Indeed, some Bible translations even insert the word 'Place' after 'Most Holy'. It is true that this is what this phrase refers to elsewhere in the Old Testament. The Jerusalem Temple Sanctuary is called the 'Most Holy' or the 'Holy of Holies' in many Jewish texts. However, if there is evidence in the passage that a word is not being used in its traditional sense, that *contextual* evidence ought to take precedence over known tradition in determining the word's meaning. Where such contextual evidence exists, scholars ought *not* to be insisting on the more common meaning of the word (its meaning in other Jewish texts). As we shall now see, the contextual evidence in Daniel 9:24-25 favours the view that the Most Holy is a *person*, not a place.

Daniel 9:24 (p.17) lists certain activities that the Jews and the city of Jerusalem were to complete within the 'Seventy 'sevens'' that the prophecy refers to. The last of these is to '*anoint* the Most Holy'. If the 'Most Holy' were intended to be the Temple Sanctuary, what could this phrase possibly mean? Anointing (generally by pouring scented oil onto someone) was usually something done to a person, not a place. Although Exodus 40:9 does command the anointing of holy objects, one would expect that to have been common practice in the Temple, not something reserved for those seventy 'sevens'. So could the word translated 'anoint' be a metaphor for 'cleanse' or 'rededicate' as many claim?

As far as I can see, the very next verse rules this out (or at least makes it extremely improbable). Verse 25 refers to 'an Anointed One' who would be an *exalted leader'* (a 'king' or 'ruler' or 'prince' – see * p.37). The fact that an anointing is referred to in the previous verse makes it *quite unreasonable* to claim that the Anointed One in verse 25 (p.17) is not the receiver of the anointing that the previous verse refers to. Hence the 'Most Holy' that gets anointed in verse 24 ought to be identified as the Anointed One in verse 25. And unless the term translated 'Most Holy' can be interpreted in a plural way (the word 'Most' suggests it can't), the Anointed One who gets 'put to death' in verse 26 (p.18) has to be one-and-the-same as the Anointed One referred to in verse 25.

The logic of this argument is so straightforward I can only surmise that scholars' insistence on the Most Holy being the Temple Sanctuary is purely an attempt to distance themselves from the conservative (Christian) claim that this phrase refers to Jesus Christ. It has, however, caused much confusion about the meaning of the verses that follow. There is constant debate over whether the 'seven 'sevens' and sixty-two 'sevens'' of the time period are meant to constitute a single interval of 'sixty-nine 'sevens'' (expressed poetically like 'four and twenty' or 'three score and ten'), or else a time period that was meant to predict the arrival of *two anointed ones* (one after the first seven 'sevens', and the other after the sixty-two that follow). Some even argue for the possibility that the seven 'sevens' is the first seven *of* the 'sixty-two 'sevens'' – a view that conveniently knocks forty-nine years off of the embarrassingly long time period, which is still far too long to end anywhere near the time the book of Daniel was completed.

All these alternatives to a continuous time period of sixty-nine 'sevens' (483 years) are totally ruled out by the conclusion that the Most Holy *to be anointed* in verse 24 (p.17) is the *Anointed One* in verse 25 – a conclusion very strongly implied by the proximity of this instance of '*Anointed* One' to that mention of a particular *anointing*. That is because it means there is only one Anointed One being referred to. Since sixty-two 'sevens' (434 years) is far longer than a human lifetime, that person can't possibly appear after the seven 'sevens' and then die after the sixty-two. Hence the only reasonable view of the prophecy is that it predicts **the coming of a single Anointed One (an exalted leader who would soon be put to death) at the end of sixty-nine 'sevens' after Nehemiah received his permission to rebuild Jerusalem**.

That is the only justifiable interpretation of this prophecy because, remember, **the prayer that precedes it has so much in common with the first prayer in the book of Nehemiah** that it was almost certainly derived from that well-known source. And that prayer of Nehemiah's is immediately followed by his account of the issuing of his **permission to rebuild Jerusalem,** making it inconceivable that the writer of Daniel 9 did not have that permission on his mind when he made this prophecy of Jerusalem's rebuilding the answer to Daniel's prayer. Let us now look at history to see just how accurate this genuine prediction turned out to be.

NOTES RELATING TO CHAPTER 5

* The Hebrew word which I have rendered 'exalted leader or king' is *Nagid,* which wasn't the usual word for 'king' (*Melek*). This is why it is translated 'ruler' or 'prince' in most Bibles. However, to my mind this gives the false impression that *Nagid* denotes a lower and more common class of leader than *Melek*. On the contrary, in the Old Testament *Nagid* appears to have been reserved for relatively rare popular leaders, whether kings, princes, or high priests; particularly those believed to be 'exalted' or 'raised up' by God. It is therefore perfectly applicable to the triumphant Christ.

At the descent of the Mount of Olives,
the whole multitude of the disciples began to rejoice
and praise God with a loud voice
for all the mighty works which they had seen, saying,
"Blessed is the King who comes in the name of the Lord!
Peace in heaven, and glory in the highest!"
Some of the Pharisees from the multitude said to him,
"Teacher, rebuke your disciples!"
He answered them, "I tell you, if these were silent,
the stones would cry out."
When he came near, he saw the city and wept over it, saying,
"If you, even you, had known today
the things which belong to your peace!
But now, they are hidden from your eyes.
For the days will come on you,
when your enemies will throw up a barricade against you,
surround you, hem you in on every side,
and will dash you and your children within you to the ground.
They will not leave in you one stone on another,
because you didn't know the time of your visitation."

Luke 19:37-44 (The Triumphal Entry of Jesus to Jerusalem)

6. The Amazing Accuracy of Daniel 9:24-25

As the conservative scholar and Scotland Yard detective Sir Robert Anderson observed in *The Coming Prince* (1894), the concept of 'year' implicit in the word 'seven' in Daniel 9 is very likely to be *360 days* (twelve 30-day months). That was a very common idea of the year's length in the ancient Middle East (which is probably why there are 360 degrees in a full turn), and there is evidence in Daniel 12 that the writer of Daniel himself thought of long periods of time in terms of a repeating unit of 360 days (see # p.44).

The amazing thing is that when one thus considers each 'seven' to be 'seven times 360 days', **the sixty-nine 'sevens'** *exactly spans the number of months* **(possibly even the number of** *days***) from the issuing of Nehemiah's permission in early March 444 BC until the most likely date for the Triumphal Entry of Jesus of Nazareth (the only person widely known as the** *Anointed One* **– the Christ), which was late March 33 AD**. This astonishing fact was pointed out by Harold Hoehner in *Chronological Aspects of the Life of Christ* (1973), who was essentially updating Anderson's work (see * p.44). Whilst scholars in Anderson's day dated Nehemiah's Permission to 445 BC, Hoehner observed that there is now far more evidence for the 444 BC date, and thus the prediction of a Christ in 33 AD (the year most strongly supported by the gospels).

The reason for the confusion is that scholars dating this event weren't taking into account the fact that Nehemiah was reckoning the king's regnal years on a calendar where the first month of the year was *Tishri* (September/October), rather than on the one used by the Persian kings, and later Jews, in which the first month is *Nisan* (March/April) – see Hoehner 1977, p.127. As Hoehner rightly points out, this is by far the best explanation for the fact that, in the book of Nehemiah, the month of *Chislev* (November/December) occurs *before* the month of Nisan (March/April) in Artaxerxes' twentieth year, as Nehemiah 1:1 and 2:1 clearly imply (p.23). Since Artaxerxes I began to reign in December 465 BC, his twentieth year on Nehemiah's calendar – the twentieth calendar year in which he reigned – would not be finished until the first day of the month of Tishri in 444 BC. Hence the month of Nisan in which Nehemiah received his permission to rebuild Jerusalem has to be that of 444 BC. Hoehner also notes that the same calendar was being used by the Jews of Elephantine in Egypt around the same time. In view of this evidence, it is amazing how often the date of Nehemiah's permission is given as 445 BC. As far as I can see, scholars who give that date cannot be taking this evidence into account. They must simply be interpreting 'the month of Nisan in the twentieth year of Artaxerxes' (Nehemiah 2:1) as Nisan 445 BC as it would be if Nehemiah were using the Nisan-to-Nisan calendar, which he almost certainly was not.

Hoehner also noted that the date of 33 AD for Christ's crucifixion is by far the one best supported by the evidence in the gospels. His arguments for this are very persuasive. So provided you accept the March 444 BC date for Nehemiah's permission, his sixty-nine 'sevens' almost certainly does lead *precisely* to the time of Christ's Triumphal Entry (the day after his anointing according to John 12).

Hoehner made one small mistake though. He forgot to take account of the fact that his dates for Nehemiah's Permission and the Triumphal Entry were *Julian* calendar dates (rather than

Gregorian ones). His method of calculation would only work accurately if they had been Gregorian ones. Consequently, he overextended that time period by about *four days* due to the century rule for leap years that the Julian calendar does not contain. Since only the month of Nehemiah's permission is given in the Old Testament, this makes no difference to the accuracy of the fulfilment. In fact, it probably makes it more believable due to the fact that it does not demand the issuing of Nehemiah's letters on the very first day of the month of Nisan. However, it also pushes Hoehner's date for the first day of that month back into late February on the Gregorian calendar. Since all the months occur at the same time of year or season on the Gregorian calendar, this is rather early for the Jewish month of Nisan. Since records began that month has always started in either Gregorian March or Gregorian April due to the need to ensure there was sufficient food for the Passover Feast on its 15th day.

It is important to remember, though, that this observation *does not by any means rule out* Hoehner's date for Nehemiah's permission. Whatever calendar he was using could easily have got out of step with the seasons by a full month or so. That was *not uncommon* in ancient times. Although the Jews were in the habit of correcting theirs before this could happen to ensure there was sufficient food for their Passover Feast, a milder winter could easily have allowed an early Nisan. Moreover, one must not forget that Nehemiah was in Babylon when he received his letters, not Jerusalem. The Jews in Babylon might have happily started their month of Nisan before hearing from Jerusalem that Nisan was to be postponed that year. Nehemiah perhaps forgot to amend his notes – or chose to use the Babylonian date of his letters – when he wrote his memoir later on.

What is not widely recognised is that there are only *three* plausible meanings for the word 'year' implicit in the meaning of 'seven', as it would have been understood by Jewish readers in 165 BC. One is the solar or *lunisolar* 'calendar cycle', which makes the sixty-nine 'sevens' approximately 483 *solar years* (plus or minus a month or so). Another is the 364-day years of exactly fifty-two weeks that some Jewish sects promoted. And the third is the 360-day years of exactly twelve full 30-day months that we have been discussing. **The fact that one of these just happens to precisely span the interval of time between one of the very small number of *days* on which Nehemiah could have received his permission to rebuild Jerusalem and the most plausible day for Christ's Triumphal Entry, just as a perfect historical fulfilment of this prophecy requires, is indeed an astonishing discovery**. It is a coincidence that was incredibly unlikely to happen by chance. But just in case the requirement of 360-day years makes you not so certain of this, let us now work out exactly *how* unlikely it was.

As we have seen, '360 days' is one of only *three* plausible meanings for the repeating unit of time that is implicit in the meaning of the word 'seven' that the prophecy uses. Allowing Nehemiah to receive his permission any time in the month of Nisan in 444 BC, and granting that the 30 days of Nisan in 445 BC is also a possibility (an unlikely one in my opinion since it would require the word for 'twentieth' in Nehemiah 1:1 to have accidentally replaced the word for 'nineteenth'), means there are only 120 possible *days* for the starting point of this time period (the 60 days of the two possible months of Nisan, multiplied by two to account for the two possible *positions* of that month relative to the seasons). Now let's take into account the three plausible meanings for the word 'seven' in the prophecy. Since each of these would make the time period finish within a separate 120 days, we can conclude that there are only 3 times 120 days (360 days *in total*) on which that time period could plausibly have ended. To fulfil this prophecy as far as our current knowledge of history allows us to verify, a famous Anointed One – a famous *Christ* – had to arrive at Jerusalem, be proclaimed 'king' (or 'exalted leader') and subsequently get killed empty-handed, on one of only 360 specific days in the whole of history. What is the chance of that happening?

In the 2180 years since that prophecy is known to have been written down, there has so far only been *one* famous Christ who was proclaimed 'king' at Jerusalem and then killed empty handed. (I am here discounting the second century Jewish leader Bar Kokhba on the grounds that we don't know whether or not he was proclaimed 'king' at Jerusalem – a city that was in ruins at the start of his leadership). Since 360 days is roughly one year, we can therefore estimate the probability of this fulfilment of prophecy as *less than one out of 2180*. But how can we *understand* this probability? Assuming that it is *exactly* one out of 2180, we can understand this as meaning that we should only expect one out of every 2180 *prophecies of the same event with a different time period* to prove true (to the limits of our current knowledge). As far as I am aware, there are in existence few, if any, prophecies of this event utilising a different time period. Consequently, the fulfilment of this one to the extent that our current knowledge of history reveals is *extremely* unlikely to have happened by chance.

But what does this *mean*? What it should mean for a scientific scholar is that perhaps this prophecy was fulfilled *on purpose*. Perhaps after it was made public around 165 BC it became so famous that people worked out when the Anointed One (the Christ) was predicted to arrive, and some even tried to become that person. Maybe Jesus of Nazareth was just the one whose attempted fulfilment of this prediction proved to be successful.

I find it intriguing to note that had Jesus made his Triumphal Entry at the end of 483 *calendar* years after Nehemiah's permission, the claim that he deliberately chose to fulfil this prediction would be a very persuasive one. It is the fact that he arrived at the end of 483 years *of exactly 360 days* that makes the fulfilment of this prediction utterly mysterious. That is because it is hard to imagine how someone without sufficiently precise knowledge of the solar year's length could have determined when that was, and **such knowledge was not widely available at that time**.

So was it just an amazing coincidence? That appears to be the only non-supernatural explanation left. However, we have not yet considered the rest of the prophecy. As you will see shortly, the most justifiable interpretation of another very specific prediction in this passage appears to have also been accurately fulfilled – which is not something one would expect if the fulfilment of the first prediction were purely chance. Intriguingly, that other fulfilment of prophecy also involves a famous wall-builder, and begins with *a word to restore and rebuild Jerusalem*. It even depends on a time-period that could be correct *to the day* if a 'seven' is 7 × 360 days!

NOTES AND CALCULATIONS RELATING TO CHAPTER 6

1290 days (Dan 12:11, p.124)=3.5 × **360 days** + one 30-day intercalary month.
  1335 days (Dan 12:12)=3.5 × **360 days** + two and a half 30-day months.

* On the lunisolar calendar popular with the Jews, each month was either 30 or 29 days long and started with the new moon. The Passover Feast was held at the *full* moon in the springtime month of Nisan (the first month of the year – though not for Nehemiah whose calendar almost certainly began with Tishri). Due to the fact that the lunar year is just over 354 days, Nisan would begin 11 days earlier every year. Consequently, when its starting date was judged to be too near the winter to allow crops to ripen in time for the Passover feast, an extra month was added to the previous year (or perhaps to the *same* year in the case of Nehemiah – the method of intercalation his calendar used is not known).

Hoehner assumed that Nehemiah's permission to rebuild Jerusalem was issued on 1st Nisan in 444 BC (though only 'the *month* of Nisan' is stated in Nehemiah 2:1). Using lunar tables, he dated this to March 5th (on the Julian calendar). He also dated the 15th Nisan in 33 AD (the date of the Passover, and the day after the crucifixion) as April 4th using lunar tables, and he used the account in John's gospel to claim that the Triumphal Entry took place on Monday 30th March 33 AD. However, his calculation of the number of days between these dates was erroneous. To ensure we have the exact number of days, the best way is to use a calendar converter to change the proposed start and end dates to

Julian day numbers (the number of days that have passed since noon on the Julian calendar date of January 1ˢᵗ 4713 BC). Thus March 5ᵗʰ 444 BC = **1559316** and March 30ᵗʰ 33 AD = **1733200**. We can then just do a simple subtraction and compare the answer with the number of days in the 69 "sevens" (which is 69 × 7 × 360 = 173880 days). The number of days between our two dates is thus

1733200 − 1559316 = 173884 days;

which means that if the time period has to start on 1ˢᵗ Nisan (March 5ᵗʰ) 444 BC, it falls short of the Triumphal Entry in 33 AD by *only 4 days!*

Of course, since only the *month* of Nisan is stated in Nehemiah 2:1, the time period *doesn't* need to start on 1ˢᵗ Nisan. In my opinion the most obvious starting point would be the date on the letters Nehemiah requested, which could easily have been 5ᵗʰ Nisan (March 9ᵗʰ 444 BC, assuming the not-too-implausible early start for Nisan in Babylon that Hoehner proposes). This would make the time period end *precisely* on the most probable date for the Triumphal Entry .

Whatever you think of the assumptions in this calculation, the unappreciated *certainty* of the starting date (it has to be *Nisan* in *444 BC* because of the similarities of Daniel's prayer to that of Nehemiah), and the very few options for the unit of time, makes it utterly astonishing that it is even possible. Although other attempts have been made to make that time period point to particular events in the life of Christ, or during the reign of Antiochus Epiphanes, none of these are relevant to this discussion because they do not take Nehemiah's permission to rebuild Jerusalem as the starting point. They are therefore not interpreting the prophecy in the way its intended readers were most likely to interpret it. And in view of the abundant evidence that the writer of Daniel 9 was drawing inspiration from Nehemiah 1 (see chapter 4), they are also not interpreting the prophecy in the way in which that writer interpreted it. The fact that he almost certainly derived his prayer from the one to which Nehemiah attributed his royal permission to rebuild Jerusalem, makes it unreasonable to think that he did not regard Daniel's 'word to restore and rebuild Jerusalem' as that royal permission. Besides, the Triumphal Entry is easily the historical event that *best* fits the end-point's description: 'Christ, an exalted leader or king'.

When, therefore, you see the abomination of desolation,
which was spoken of through the prophet Daniel,
standing in the holy place (let the reader understand),
then let those who are in Judea flee to the mountains.
Let him who is on the housetop not go down
to take out the things that are in his house.
Let him who is in the field not return back to get his clothes.
But woe to those who are with child
and to nursing mothers in those days!
Pray that your flight will not be in the winter, nor on a Sabbath,
for then there will be great oppression,
such as has not been from the beginning of the world until now,
no, nor ever will be.
Unless those days had been shortened,
no flesh would have been saved.
But for the sake of the chosen ones,
those days will be shortened.

Matthew 24:15-22 [also in Mark 13:14-20] (Christ on Daniel 9:27)

You shall count off seven Sabbaths of years, seven times seven years;
to you will be the days of seven Sabbaths of years, even forty-nine years.
Then you shall sound the loud trumpet…You shall make the fiftieth year
holy, and proclaim liberty throughout the land to all its inhabitants.
It shall be a jubilee to you…In it you shall not sow, nor reap…

Leviticus 25:8-11 (The Jubilee Year Cycle)

7. What comes *after* the Anointed One?

Walking along Hadrian's wall on a hot summer's day in the 80s, I heard much about that roaming emperor. But nobody told me he was predicted in the Bible. In chapter 6, we saw that Daniel 9:25 predicts the arrival at Jerusalem (and later execution) of an exalted Christ at the end of *'seven "sevens" and sixty-two "sevens"'* from the day Nehemiah received his permission to rebuild Jerusalem. I find it utterly astonishing that one of only three plausible meanings of that very long time period ends within at most a month of the likeliest date for the Triumphal Entry of Jesus Christ – the only really famous Christ in history. That time period was 5796 30-day months long, for goodness sake! It wasn't likely to finish *anywhere near* the Jerusalem arrival of a Christ who'd be widely regarded as 'most holy' and 'exalted leader'. Of course, the slight uncertainty over the relevant dates means this is really a *potential* fulfilment. In contrast, the accuracy of the *next* prediction in the passage is not in any kind of doubt. The final two verses of the prophecy say this:

> **Dan 9:26-27** [26]After the sixty-two "sevens", the Anointed One [the 'Christ'] will be put to death and will have nothing. **The people of *the ruler who will come* [another *'exalted leader or king'*] will destroy the city and the sanctuary.** His end will be

with a flood. War will go on until the end, and desolations are determined. **²⁷He will confirm a covenant with many for one "seven". In the middle of the "seven" he will cause the sacrifice and the offering to cease. And on an *overspreading* [or *'wing'*] he will set up the abomination of desolation, even until the full end, that which is determined, is poured out on him.** [Or: 'on the wing of abominations will come one who makes desolate, even until a full end…is poured out on him (or 'on *it (the desolate)'*, which makes very little sense).']

As we saw in chapter 3, this was definitely intended to be a prediction. There is no good reason to think this was meant to be about events that had happened shortly before the book of Daniel was completed, as all critical scholars currently maintain. These events are clearly predicted (from hindsight) in both Daniel 8 and Daniel 11, and this fact would have necessitated the inclusion of prophecies that genuinely predicted the future in order to stop the book of Daniel being rejected as a forgery. Since its intended readers would have had no trouble recognising that the time period in this prophecy placed the events it predicts well into their distant future, this has to be one of those genuine predictions. **The fact that some of the events it predicts resemble those of Daniel 11 is irrelevant because the writer of the book of Daniel had good reason to choose a prophecy for this purpose that contained such resemblances**. Those resemblances would attract attention to it, thereby enabling its predictive nature to be discovered.

As we have seen, the time for the coming of the Anointed One (the Christ) was fulfilled by the Triumphal Entry of Jesus (by far the most famous Christ in history). And as everyone knows, Jesus was put to death shortly afterwards, empty-handed, just as this passage predicts. But did the people of a 'ruler who will come' destroy the city and sanctuary sometime after this event? And if so, was that ruler's end *'the end determined'* (that of the 70 'sevens' of v.24)? Did he die (v.27) *seven years after he began to fulfil a public vow?*

Since the prophecy is about Daniel's *people and holy city* (see v.24, p.17), 'the city and the sanctuary' definitely means Jerusalem and her Temple. Consequently, verse 26 says that both these places would be destroyed sometime after the death of Christ by a people whose ruler would personally visit the Jerusalem site. Of course, that on its own is not a particularly *specific* prediction. Jerusalem was bound to get destroyed at some point after 3rd April 33 AD, and her Temple would very probably be razed to the ground at the same time. It is also fairly likely that a ruler of the people who destroyed it would choose to visit the site of such a great conquest.

Hence it is perhaps not all that surprising that these things did indeed come to pass. In 70 AD the Roman armies of the emperor Vespasian, led by his son and successor Titus, destroyed the city of Jerusalem and burned down the Jewish Temple. However, whilst both Vespasian and Titus visited Jerusalem, neither is known to have done so *in the capacity of Emperor*, as a fulfilment of this prediction would seem to require. Moreover, the deeds of 'the ruler who will come' in verse 27 seem a far cry from what is known of Vespasian or Titus. *They* didn't keep a covenant for seven years or end Jewish sacrifice *within four years of their deaths*. Vespasian died in 79 and Titus in 81 – each more than *eight* years after the Temple's destruction interrupted Jewish sacrifice and offering.

Another detail worth considering is the fact that the prophecy predicts the destruction of Jerusalem by '*the people of* the ruler who will come'. Normally such an act would be attributed directly to the commander in the field. The fact that it says 'the people of' here is most reasonably interpreted as meaning that the 'ruler who will come' will not be present at the time Jerusalem gets destroyed.

So is there a powerful Roman ruler (the Hebrew word means 'exalted leader') who was not present when the Roman armies destroyed Jerusalem in 70 AD, but who later visited the Jerusalem site and there made a promise to many people that he confirmed *for a seven-year period ending with his death*, in the middle of which he put a final stop to Jewish sacrifice and offering, and set up an idol for worship on an infamous overspreading?

Amazingly, the answer is YES! In around 130 AD the Roman Emperor Hadrian, famous for travelling all over his vast empire to see it with his own eyes, visited the site of Jerusalem, which still lay in ruins after its destruction in 70 AD. There he appears to have promised the Jewish people he would rebuild it. (Notice that a promise *to rebuild Jerusalem* is the most likely meaning of 'covenant' in the context of this passage). The building work most probably commenced in 131 AD. The exact date of the foundation ceremony is currently unknown, but since Hadrian's plans for the city were the cause of a war that definitely erupted in 132 AD, it was most probably sometime in the summer of 131. As a result of Hadrian's plan to dedicate the city to himself and the Roman God *Jupiter Capitolinus*, the Jews rebelled. They were at first success-ful. But by the end of 134 the tide had turned against them. Their leader Simon Bar Kokhba (an epithet meaning 'son of the star') was finally defeated in the summer of 135, and the remaining resistance destroyed by the spring of the following year. Hadrian then made Jerusalem off-limits for Jews, and massacred the Judean population in very large numbers. He renamed their now-desolate land 'Syria Palestina' after their traditional enemies, and had an equestrian statue and shrine to himself (an 'abomination' to Jews) erected upon the site of the Jerusalem Temple. He also had that site infamously *ploughed over* in a sacrilegious act commemorated on Roman coins and remembered with hatred in subsequent Jewish tradition. Incredibly, he even died of disease in the summer of 138 – *exactly seven years after his re-founding of Jerusalem in 131!*

We can be fairly certain the founding of Hadrian's new Jerusalem (Aelia Capitolina) was in 131 because it had to precede the start of the war in 132 and follow Hadrian's visit to the region in 130. The Roman Historian Cassius Dio, writing a few decades later, tells us:

At Jerusalem, he founded a city in place of the one which had been razed to the ground, naming it Aelia Capitolina, and on the site of the temple of the god, he raised a new temple to Jupiter. This brought on a war of no slight importance nor of brief duration, for the Jews deemed it intolerable that foreign races should be settled in their city and foreign religious rites planted there.. Very few of them in fact survived.. Five hundred and eighty thousand men were slain.. and the number of those that perished by famine, disease and fire was past finding out. Thus nearly all Judaea was made desolate' *(Roman History 69:12)*

The foundation ceremony – the moment Hadrian began *confirming* his promise – has to come after his arrival in 130 AD, and has to precede the outbreak of war by at least a few months to account for the building work to which Dio attributes that catastrophe. Hence 130 and 131 are the only reasonable possibilities, with 131 being more likely. It is interesting to note that since scholars are fairly certain Hadrian died on 10th July 138 AD, any future discovery dating that foundation ceremony to mid-August 131 would not only be dramatic confirmation of the accuracy of this prediction, but it would demand that the 'sevens' are indeed interpreted as periods of 'seven times 360 days' as Christ's fulfilment of the earlier part of the prophecy requires. Intriguingly, rabbinical sources claim that it took place on the ninth of the Jewish month of *Av*. In 131 that fell in either mid-July or (amazingly) mid-August! The fact that Hadrian was in nearby Egypt in the winter of 130-131 mourning the death of his lover Antinous actually favours the latter since it would've made the Jews eager to delay their festive season.

But even without that confirmation, Hadrian's fulfilment of this prediction is stunning. Not only did he die seven years after confirming his covenant to rebuild Jerusalem, but he also put a final end to Jewish sacrifice and offering (see * p.54) midway through those seven years, just as 'the ruler who will come' in the prophecy does. His banning of the Jews from Jerusalem ensured that no more Jewish sacrifices could be performed at their Temple site. Although one could quibble that this was slightly *beyond* the mid-point of that 'seven', it seems clear to me that the ending of sacrifice and offering really took place around the beginning of 135 when the Jews no longer had any hope of victory. That was bang on the mid-point. The important observation here is that *since that time* the Jews have never been able to resume their sacrifice and offering in Jerusalem. Not for *one thousand eight hundred and eighty years* and counting. That is truly extraordinary.

But Hadrian's fulfilment of this prophecy goes even further than that. In founding Aelia, he had his governor *plough over* the Temple site, and he later raised a statue and shrine to himself there. That ploughing, which is portrayed on Roman coins, constituted a sacrilegious act that was remembered with great hatred in Jewish tradition. It is therefore simply astonishing that 'the ruler who will come' in Daniel 9:27 is predicted to set up an 'abomination of desolation' – a term clearly meaning 'foreign idol' in Daniel 11:31 – *'on an **overspreading**'*. As you can see, the word 'overspreading' (often translated 'wing') could very easily refer to a ***ploughing over*** – a highly appropriate word for the Temple site at that time.

I find Hadrian's fulfilment of this prediction spookily precise. Although there is some disagreement amongst translators over whether this verse refers to an 'abomination of desolation' or an 'overspreading of abominations', I think the use of the former phrase in Daniel 11:31 to describe the idol set up by Antiochus Epiphanes weighs heavily in favour of that being the intended translation of Daniel 9:27. The writer has chosen that phrase to describe Epiphanes' recent actions as a means of drawing attention to this prophecy. He has done this so that his readers would take an interest in this rather less-detailed prophecy. He was hoping they'd wonder whether it might also be about Antiochus Epiphanes and take a good look at it as a result. Provided he could persuade them to do this, he was confident that they would realise that the time period it contains sets its predicted 'abomination of desolation' **a long time after Epiphanes established his**. That would quash any suspicion that the book of Daniel was purely concerned with those recent events, thereby giving them ammunition to defend the book against those astute skeptics who were calling it a forgery.

And just in case this prophecy happened to have genuinely come from God, he left its wording pretty much as he had found it (though perhaps translating it from Aramaic into Hebrew to reduce the number of times his book changed between different languages). That is why, in Daniel 9:27, the Abomination of Desolation is set up 'on an overspreading' rather than 'in the sanctuary' as is implied by Daniel 11:31. It is also why Daniel 9:26 has the sanctuary being *destroyed*, along with the city of Jerusalem, *more than three years before* an abomination is set up, whereas in Daniel 11:31 the sanctuary is described as being 'profaned' rather than destroyed, and the raising of the abomination of desolation is mentioned in the same verse with no long intervening time period suggested (see p.123). These details strongly support this prediction hypothesis. But perhaps the best evidence for it is the fact that in 33 AD Christ himself referred to Daniel's Abomination of Desolation as a future event (see Mark 13 and Matthew 24, p.46). He said it would herald *the worst ever oppression in Judea* – which Hadrian's massacres probably were!

Let's remember, though: Even if this text *wasn't* intended as a prediction, it should still astound us. The fact that future events fulfilled its plainest meaning wouldn't be any *less* bizarre and surprising if that meaning were an accident: the result of a writer's poor grasp of history or language, or lack of concern for accuracy. As we have seen, mainstream scholars attribute the inconsistencies between this passage and the portrayals of Epiphanes in Daniel 8 and Daniel 11 to an extremely unlikely mix *of exceptionally weak chronology* (the time period), *overly ambitious numerical symbolism* ('seventy'), *exaggerations* ('destroy'), and *literary* *ineptitude*. They claim it was an attempt to create the impression of a prophecy gradually becoming clearer as the book of Daniel progresses. Even if they were correct in doing this, the fact that the resultant prophecy perfectly predicts the death of Jesus Christ, the destruction of Jerusalem in 70 AD, and the anti-Jewish activities of Hadrian – including his ending of Jewish sacrifice and offering* and the timing of his death – would still be absolutely amazing.

Nevertheless, for the purpose of understanding the content of the book of Daniel, it is important to note that there is no justification for that mainstream story. The similarity of the prayer in Daniel 9 to the prayer in Nehemiah 1 (ch.4) clearly indicates that the writer regarded Nehemiah's permission to rebuild Jerusalem as the start of the time period in the prophecy; and if so, *he couldn't possibly have meant Daniel 9 to be a cloudy prediction of Antiochus Epiphanes*. Besides, there is no good reason why he should *want* to include another prophecy of Epiphanes in this book. He already had two perfectly satisfactory ones in the form of Daniel 8 and Daniel 11. Since he obviously wanted to pass this book off as 'the recently discovered work of an ancient prophet', what he desperately needed was to include predictions that extended further into the future than his own time. Without such predictions his intended readers were bound to dismiss the book as a forgery. Since those intended readers were sure to realise that in their day this prophecy did indeed predict distant future events, we have no reason to think that this was not its purpose. Interestingly, though, Daniel 9 is not the only accurate prophecy in the book of Daniel to which this astonishing conclusion applies.

NOTES RELATING TO CHAPTER 7

* Jewish sacrifice and offering appears not to have been completely stopped by the destruction of the Temple in 70 AD (see K. W. Clark, 'Worship in the Jerusalem Temple after A.D. 70', *NTS* 6(4), 1960, 269-280), and was very likely encouraged under Bar Kokhba in 132 (see Wilson 1989, p.81; Jerome, p.109).

8. The Four Monsters of Daniel 7

Fifty-three miles south of modern-day Baghdad lies the site of the ancient city of Babylon. There, around 553 BC, the prophet Daniel reportedly had the dream we now find in Daniel 7. Several decades earlier, he and thousands of Jews had been forcibly resettled in that region by Nebuchadnezzar II, the king of Babylon who destroyed Jerusalem and her Temple in 587 BC (and who gets humbled by God in Daniel 4). Under that king, Babylon had expanded into an empire stretching from Iraq all the way to the borders of Egypt; and the city had become a magnificent seat of power. Although Nebuchadnezzar was long dead by 553 BC, **Babylon** under his successors still dominated the Middle East. However, all that was about to change. The Median Empire to the north had once been an ally of Babylon. But by this time its king had grown extremely unpopular with his nobles. In the next couple of years, a rebellious faction of the Median nobility would invite his grandson Cyrus, king of the Persian state of Anshan, a region subordinate to the Median throne, to take over. And unlike his Median predecessors, the ambitious Cyrus would not be content with mere alliances.

Having successfully usurped the Median throne in 550 BC, sparing his unpopular grandad's life, Cyrus and his Median generals would go on to unleash their **Medo-Persian** forces in successful wars of conquest against the neighbouring states. By 546 BC the powerful and famously wealthy kingdom of Lydia had fallen. Surprisingly, its king Croesus was spared and added to Cyrus' retinue of advisors – a risky act of royal mercy that was extremely unusual in those violent times. Then in 539 BC the forces of Cyrus (led by his general Gobryas, who may be the controversial 'Darius the Mede' of Daniel 5-6) took Babylon itself. They killed its king Belshazzar; but according to ancient Babylonian sources, his father and co-ruler Nabonidus became **a third defeated king to be treated well**.

Cyrus' Persian successors went on to annex Egypt and dominate the world for the next two centuries. They looked after the interests of large minorities to gain their support, and the Jews were thus able to return and rebuild their temple, and eventually – following the permission granted to Nehemiah – reconstruct Jerusalem.

But the days of Persian dominance were numbered. They came to an abrupt end in 331 BC when the last Persian emperor was decisively conquered by the **Greek** (Macedonian) king, Alexander the Great, who went on to carve out further territories as far away as India, before dying mysteriously in Babylon in 323 BC.

In the protracted power struggle that Alexander's untimely death gave rise to, his Greek empire split into **four separate Greek kingdoms** ruled by the heads of **four contemporaneous dynasties** (the *Ptolemies, Seleucids, Antigonids* and *Attalids*), and it remained that way well into the second century BC. It's worth noting that four large power-bases were first decided upon by Alexander's generals in 311 BC as a means of governing his empire in the name of his heir – his son Alexander IV (born shortly after his death). He also had a half-brother called Philip who had by then been executed. That one remaining heir was, however, eventually murdered too, and those generals then declared themselves kings, fighting each other (along with invading Celts) in an attempt to re-unite the empire. Although three of them subsequently fell, in each case a new Greek general took over, until the succession stabilised into the same four enduring kingdoms. However, despite the fact that two of these constituted large empires capable of fielding vast armies, they were no match for the professional legions of **Rome**. All four had submitted to the might of Rome by **189 BC**.

The last to do so was the Seleucid Empire that ruled over the Jews in Judea. Its forces were soundly crushed by a Roman commander in January 189 BC at the battle of Magnesia in Asia Minor. From then on its kings – including the villainous Antiochus Epiphanes – spent their early years as hostages of the Roman Senate. When in 171 BC the Antigonid kingdom of Macedon, the home territory of Alexander himself, rebelled, the response of Rome was swift and decisive. After defeating the rebellious king, the Romans removed his family from power, and as a lesson to the other Greek kingdoms **broke his territory up** into four independent republics.

Writing in 165 BC, shortly after this powerful reassertion of Rome's dominance, the writer of the book of Daniel appears to have been well aware of these events. Daniel 11, for example, clearly alludes to Rome's crushing victory over the Seleucid state; and it also mentions an episode where Antiochus Epiphanes was humiliatingly forced to abandon one of his conquests on the orders of a Roman ambassador right in front of his army (see Appendix p.125). In the light of this, what do you think that writer might have meant by the following dream imagery (Daniel 7:1-7)? How would his intended readers be *most likely* to understand it?

> **Dan 7:1-4** [1]In the first year of Belshazzar king of Babylon Daniel had a dream...[2]..."I saw in my night vision and, behold, the four winds of heaven broke out on the great sea. [3]**Four great beasts rose from the sea, different from one another.**
>
> [4]The first was **like a *lion*, and had eagle's wings**. As I looked its wings were plucked, and it was lifted up from the earth, and made to stand on two feet as a man. It was given a man's heart.

Later we learn that these four beasts stand for *four ruling kingdoms* – i.e. *empires*. And this first one (a lion) can only be the Empire of **Babylon** that ruled the Middle East at the time of the dream. We know this because there's another prophecy in the book of Daniel (Daniel 2) that clearly predicts the same four empires, and the first in that vision is distinctly identified as Babylon (v.38, p.70). Note however that the features of this beast symbolise *recognisable features* of Babylon. The winged lion was typical of Babylonian art, and its transformation reminds the reader of the humbling of Babylon's famous king recounted in Daniel 4 (see p. xiii). With this in mind, look back at the bit of history on pages 56 and 57, and see if you can identify the other three beasts described below.

> **Dan 7:5-7** [5]Behold, there was a second beast, one like a *bear*. It was **raised up on one side**, and **three ribs were in its mouth** between its teeth. They said to it: 'Arise! Devour much flesh!'
>
> [6]After this I looked, and behold, another, like a *leopard*, which had on its back **four wings of a bird.** This beast also had **four heads**; and dominion was given to it.
>
> [7]After this I looked in the night visions, and, behold, there was a fourth beast, **awesome and powerful**, and **exceedingly strong.** It had **great iron teeth.** It devoured and **broke in pieces**, and stamped the residue with its feet. It was *different from all the animals that were before it*. It had ten horns.

You may well have guessed the identity of each monster just by matching the sequence of monsters with the sequence of empires that followed Babylon. That historical sequence of empires is definitely Babylon, then Persia (or *Medo-Persia*), the empire of Cyrus the Great who conquered Babylon (and which is depicted as a single *Medo-Persian* beast in Daniel 8), then Greece, then Rome. But have you worked out what any of the *features* stand for yet? With most of them, it really isn't that difficult. Have a look at the table opposite. Was your guess the same as mine, by any chance?

HOW THE INTENDED READERS WOULD INTERPRET DANIEL 7

Winged Lion = **Babylon** (Nebuchadnezzar's Babylonian Empire)

    Man's heart = Humbling of Nebuchadnezzar (Dan 4:16)

Bear = **Medo-Persian** Empire (the conquerors of Babylon)

    Raised side = *Persians* (Cyrus and his successors)

    Lowered side = *Medes* (the lower *horn* in Dan 8:3 & 20 p.121)

    Three ribs between teeth = Three kings Cyrus spared (p.56)

    "Devour much flesh!"= Conquer many nations

Four-headed, four-winged **leopard** = **Greek** Empire of Alexander

    Four **Wings** = Four separate *successor kingdoms* (v.22 p.122)

    Four **Heads** = Four contemporaneous *ruling dynasties* (p.56)

Highly distinct Monster = **Roman** Empire (Dominant 189 BC⇦)

    Iron Teeth = Professional Legions   Horns = Future kings

    Distinctness = Republic (in 165 BC) – not a monarchy

    Break in pieces = Break-up of Macedon (167 BC)

What *else* could these animals possibly represent in 165 BC?

Surprisingly, not a single critical scholar agrees that this is what the writer of the book of Daniel intended that sequence of monsters to be. Potential sources of Daniel are even rejected as such because they support this view! Instead, they argue that the writer must have imagined that the Median Empire had conquered Babylon *before* its takeover by the Persian king Cyrus. In their view, the writer had an errant perception of history and was actually imagining the bear to stand for the pre-Cyrus *Median* Empire. They insist that the four-winged, four-headed leopard stands for *Persia* (Cyrus and his successors), and that the four-part-divided Greek empire is actually the highly distinct and exceedingly powerful *fourth* monster. They thus assume that Rome, the ruling empire of the writer's day, has been *completely ignored!*

As you have no doubt noticed, there are some majorly serious problems with this proposal. Apart from the fact that it requires the writer to have had a completely different view of what would then have been a very famous historical event (the fall of Babylon) from every other known source, it would also require him to have a different view from the one he portrays *everywhere else in the book of Daniel.* Although the king who conquers Babylon in Daniel 5 goes by the name of 'Darius the Mede', this king issues decrees that are governed by 'the law of the Medes and Persians'. This clearly shows that he was perceived as a *Medo-Persian* ruler. Moreover, in Daniel 8 – another vision of beasts – the kingdoms of Media and Persia are represented by two horns on a *single ram* (see Appendix p.122). Again we see the historical Medo-Persian Empire. This is most relevant because we know from its very clear portrayal of Antiochus Epiphanes that Daniel 8 was written around the same time as Daniel 11, and very probably by the same writer – the 165 BC compiler. Considering that the Medo-Persian ram in that chapter has *one-horn-higher-than-the-other* (representing the dominance of the Persians over the Medes), is it really reasonable to believe that this same dominance is not what the *one-side-higher-than-the-other* feature of the bear in Daniel 7 represents?

I think not. But that isn't the only evidence that contradicts this strange mainstream interpretation of those beasts. Daniel 8 also has an animal identified as 'Greece' (Alexander's empire), and like the leopard in Daniel 7, that animal (a billy goat) grows *four* of something (horns, in this case). They stand for the *four Greek kingdoms* into which Alexander's empire split. **Are we really to believe that the only animal presenting four of something in Daniel 7 was *not* meant to be that four-part-divided Greek empire? Really?**

Again I find this highly unlikely. Judging from the lion in Daniel 7 (p.58), and the ram and goat in Daniel 8 (above), the features of those beasts are meant to be *easy* to understand. It is therefore notable that most mainstream scholars admit to finding the raised stance and three ribs of the bear *'obscure'*, and they interpret the four heads and wings on the leopard (a perfect symbol of the four-part Greek empire) in an ambiguous way that never constitutes anything unique to the Persian empire they claim it represents.

In contrast, when one interprets those beasts in terms of the *known historical* sequence of empires (p.59), it is possible to match *every* feature to a unique characteristic of the empire being represented. Even the *types* of animal used have obvious meanings. The winged lion in Babylonian art was often used to represent the *Lamassu* – a spiritual guardian of the Babylonian kings. Consequently, it stands to reason that the bear and leopard also represent *spiritual guardians* of the nations they stand for (a view clearly encouraged by a reference to such guardians in Daniel 10:20). It is therefore no surprise that the Jews believed in a guardian angel of Persia called *Dobiel*, meaning *'bear god'* (see p.118). And anyone who has studied the Greek Empire will know that the leopard was a popular symbol of the Greek wine god *Dionysus*. Of all the Greek gods, Dionysus was the one most closely associated with that empire. Like Alexander the Great, he was famous for conquering India. Alexander's influential mother was a devotee; and he was widely worshipped amongst Alexander's troops. Moreover, his trademark 'mitra' headband (worn to cure his hangovers!) was thought by some to be the very inspiration for the diadem crowns that adorned the heads of Alexander's successors. Recognising this, it is no surprise that in Daniel 8 Greece is a *goat*. Like the leopard, the goat was another common symbol of Dionysus. And even the Medo-Persian ram in Daniel 8 can be equated with a guardian deity. It was one of the manifestations of the popular Zoroastrian war god *Verethragna*, and Zoroastrianism was the main *Persian* religion. The mainstream theory permits none of those equations.

We will be returning to these observations later on. Right now though, let us consider what in my view is the real killer observation for the mainstream consensus that the fourth beast in this passage is Greece. Recall that the writer of the book of Daniel was writing for Jewish readers around 165 BC. Living under one of the *four Greek kingdoms* by which Greece had for a century dominated the world – a world now into its third decade of *Roman* rule – there was no way these readers were going to think that the four heads and wings on the leopard stood for *anything other* than those four Greek kingdoms. Yet nowhere does that writer make any effort to *stop* them reaching this conclusion (which he could hardly not have anticipated). In fact, he does quite the opposite. He *encourages* them towards it by using a goat that grows four horns to represent Greece in Daniel 8 (see p.121), and by using a *single beast* – a ram in Daniel 8 – to represent the Medes *and Persians*.

Convinced that the leopard was Greece, those readers were sure to think the fourth beast was Rome. Although critical scholars often suggest that the power of Rome was somehow hidden from the Jews at that time, this is actually very unlikely. Rome's political dominance had been established by stunning military victories that returning soldiers were bound to talk about all over the Seleucid Empire. There are even allusions to these victories in the book of Daniel itself (see Daniel 11:18 – p.125). And there's also the first book of Maccabees. Written near the end of the second century

BC, 1 Maccabees 8 tells us that Judas Maccabeus, the Jewish rebel leader *at the time the book of Daniel was written*, actually sent an embassy to Rome in the summer of 161 BC. He was hoping to get Roman backing for his bid to break free from the Seleucid Empire (a struggle that went on for many years after Antiochus Epiphanes' death in 164 BC). In approaching Rome, he was just doing what other small nations had been doing over the previous three decades. Rome's dominance over the Greek kingdoms was not a new fact that nations on distant shores of the Mediterranean might not yet have heard about. It had been the political reality *for more than twenty years. Everyone* would have known about it.

The only reason critical scholars maintain this indefensible view on these monsters is because only that will allow this prophecy to be an errant prediction of recent events, as opposed to a genuine prediction of the future. You see, although there was already a fourth world-dominant empire, that empire (Rome) was a republic. She had no king. Moreover, Rome hadn't had any king since long before she gained any form of empire. Yet, the ten horns of the fourth monster (and an eleventh that rises afterwards) are interpreted as 'kings' later in the passage. Hence, judging from the fact that a horn representing Alexander the Great in Daniel 8 is identified as '*the first king*' of Greece (see Appendix p.122), those horns can only have been a prediction of *future* Roman rulers.

Critical scholars currently see this as a reason to abandon all attempts at interpreting this passage in the way its earliest readers were bound to interpret it, and settle for the view that it was just an error-riddled misperception of history. They claim that the writer was representing Epiphanes again (the *eighth* Seleucid king), and chose an *eleventh* horn (the one after the ten) purely to suggest his illegitimacy (* p.64). But the simple fact is, there isn't any reason why this prophecy *shouldn't* have been intended as a prediction of the distant future. As we saw in the case of Daniel 9, the writer of the book of Daniel had a very strong motive to include prophecies within it that would have appeared to his readers to predict events **that were still to come**. Without such passages skeptics would quickly denounce his book as a forgery. And what better way is there to make such a prophecy than to include horns representing kings on the head of a beast representing the dominant nation-state when that dominant nation-state is a centuries-old republic?

Anyway, let us now see what the prophecy says about these kings, and the fate of the kingdom they rule. In doing that we will soon discover the real reason critical scholars are so reluctant to endorse this impeccably rational explanation for the content of this passage.

NOTES RELATING TO CHAPTER 8

* Epiphanes seized power shortly after the death of his elder brother Seleucus IV, when the succession ought to have gone to Seleucus' son Demetrius, who was at that time serving as a political hostage in Rome (one of the many debasing terms of the treaty that had followed Rome's decisive victory over the Seleucid kingdom in 189 BC). Critical scholars have claimed that the number eleven was rather confusingly assigned to that eighth Seleucid king purely to suggest this illegitimacy. The far more appropriate number eight, or the number nine (for those who saw the Seleucid kings as the rightful successors of Alexander the Great), were thus supposedly rejected as not *unlucky* enough, perhaps because they were not prime numbers, or because they could be easily represented by a number of fingers. Even the number ten that might have been assigned to Epiphanes by supporters of an unsuccessful non-Seleucid usurper called Heliodorus (the 'tax collector' of Daniel 11:20, who assassinated Seleucus and tried to take over) was supposedly rejected as being unsuitable for an illegitimate monarch. They are thus claiming that the writer recklessly chose to symbolise Epiphanes as an eleventh king *even though no-one else would have recognised him as such* – not even those whose view of the Seleucid succession included Heliodorus and a murdered infant son of Seleucus IV in whose name Epiphanes first began to reign. Such people could hardly have ignored the fact that Alexander the Great's son and brother had a far greater claim than those two to be on this king list, pushing Epiphanes into *thirteenth* place.

9. Why the Eternal Kingdom has to be a New Religion

We have so far seen that Daniel 7:2-7 predicts the rise of four empires, and that the intended readers of the book of Daniel around 165 BC were *absolutely certain* to conclude that the fourth was Rome – by far the dominant nation in their day, and a centuries-old republic. Since the horns on the beast representing that empire are later said to be kings, they were sure to see this as a prophecy of Rome's future. The next five verses of this dream read as follows:

> **Dan 7:8-12** [8]I considered the horns, and behold, **there came up among them another horn, a little one, before which three of the first horns were plucked up by the roots**: and behold, in this horn were eyes like the eyes of a man, and a mouth speaking great things.
>
> [9]I watched until thrones were put in place, and one who was ancient of days took his seat. His clothing was white as snow, and the hair of his head like pure wool. His throne was fiery flames, and its wheels burning fire. [10]A fiery stream issued and came out from before him. Thousands of thousands ministered to him. Ten thousand times ten thousand stood before him. The judgment was set. The books were opened. [11]I watched at that time because of the voice of the great words which the horn

spoke. I watched even until the beast was slain, and its body destroyed, and it was given to be burned with fire. [12]As for the rest of the beasts, their dominion was taken away; **yet their lives were prolonged for a season and a time**.

Wait a minute! What on earth can the last verse here possibly have meant? As we saw in chapter 8, those four beasts stand for a succession of ruling kingdoms – empires – and when you look at the course of history evident to the writer of the book of Daniel in 165 BC (p.56-7), you will see that each was *completely conquered* by the next. Only parts of the Greek empire still survived as petty kingdoms. This immediately tells us that **the killing and burning of the fourth beast in verse 11 cannot signify the *conquest* of Rome.** After an empire's conquest, the animal representing it is still alive! And remember, neither Cyrus nor Alexander left any independent vestige of the empires they conquered in their wake. So what can those prolonged lives possibly represent?

The answer to this question will be obvious if you look back at the meaning of the **animal types** inferred earlier (p.61). Since Babylon is the Lamassu-like winged lion and Greece the Dionysian leopard, each animal type would have been identified as a *guardian deity – a religion*. As history clearly testifies, when a nation is conquered, any religion associated with it doesn't usually perish. It tends to live on for a season and a time. This was definitely the case for the Dionysian cult that this dream associates with Alexander's empire, and the Zoroastrianism of the Persians that Alexander conquered (the latter is still practiced by some today). And it was probably also the case with the ancient Babylonian belief in the Lamassu.

So what does this imply about **the killing and burning of the fourth monster** in the fire that came from the heavenly throne? Obviously, it predicts **the demise of the *Roman religion*.** This is made abundantly clear in the next six verses of Daniel 7, which describe the religion that will emerge in its place:

Dan 7:13-18 [13]I saw in the night visions, and behold, there came with the clouds of heaven **one like a son of man**, and he came even to the ancient of days, and they brought him near before him. [14]Dominion was given to him, and glory, and a kingdom, that all the peoples, nations, and languages should serve him. **His dominion is an everlasting dominion, which will not pass away, and his kingdom that which will not be destroyed.** [15]As for me, Daniel, my spirit was grieved within me, and the visions in my head troubled me. [16]I came near to one of those who stood by, and asked him the truth concerning all this. So he told me, and made me know its interpretation.

[17]**'These great animals, which are four, are four kings** [that is, *ruling kingdoms* – see v.23, p.74] **that will arise out of the earth.** [18]But the holy people of the Most High will **receive the kingdom, and possess the kingdom forever, even forever and ever.'**

As you can see, the religion predicted in this passage to completely replace the religion of Rome sometime after its eleventh king (the king represented by the eleventh horn before which three were plucked up by the roots) is one based upon a young man-like associate of the Jewish God (see * p.68). The Jewish God is obviously represented by the 'Ancient of Days' figure (verse 13) who first takes his seat upon the thrones that Daniel sees; and this 'one like a son of man' gets brought to him, before being given an everlasting kingdom to rule (verse 14). That his followers would first take over the *Roman* Empire is emphasised by verse 18. Since the last kingdom implied by verse 17 is the empire represented by the fourth monster, it is reasonable to infer that this is the kingdom that the 'holy people' receive in verse 18. And that view is further supported by the fact that it is the animal representing that empire that gets killed, while those representing the conquered empires remain alive for a time. As we noted earlier, the temporary survival of those beasts can only mean the ***continuation* of the associated religions** beyond the time of the holy people's takeover (see p.61).

The reason critical scholars never defend the fully justifiable hypothesis that Daniel 7 was included as a genuine prediction of the future of the Roman empire, is simply because **this part of it definitely came true**. A religion – Christianity – based upon worship of a young, son-of-man-like associate of the Jewish God *did indeed take over the Roman Empire sometime after its eleventh king* and *completely replaced its pagan beliefs*. Of course, this fact ought to have no bearing at all upon discussions of what the prophecy was originally intended to say. The fact that critical scholars never even consider the possibility that this passage was a genuine prediction, **despite the fact that they cannot otherwise provide any defensible account of its imagery**, is therefore strong evidence of academic bias. It strongly implies that they are ignoring this possibility in order to avoid the potential stigma of being labelled 'conservative'. As a result, the trusting public are being misled into thinking that this passage didn't really predict the rise of Christianity, **when all the evidence suggests it did**.

NOTES RELATING TO CHAPTER 9

* Critical scholars often identify this son-of-man-like figure as one of the named angels or demigods that the writer of Daniel 8 and Daniel 11 clearly believed in (usually the angel Michael who is regarded by the writer of Daniel 10-12 as the protector of the Israelites). However, what should not be in doubt is that this prophecy clearly predicts the emergence of a new religion – a religion descending from Daniel's Jewish faith, but quite distinct from it. Whoever that son-of-man-like figure represents, he is to be *served forever* by *all peoples, nations and languages*. In that, he is on a par with the Jewish God himself (represented separately in the vision by the Ancient of Days) – which means he cannot represent Israel (as some have suggested). This God-like status is further emphasised by his name. An angel in the dream refers to someone as the *Most High* – the *Highest One*. It is *his* people that receive the kingdom in verse 18. Since that verse is clearly intended to interpret the imagery of verse 14, where the 'Son of Man' is given a kingdom, we can confidently conclude that this Son of Man *is* the Most High that the angel speaks of. See also the note on page 34.

10. The Statue Dream of Daniel 2

By now you will no doubt be dying to know what the rest of Daniel 7 says, and whether the other prediction it makes (verse 8, p.65) also came true. *Did the eleventh king of the Roman Empire actually subdue three of its earlier kings*, as the reference to three horns getting uprooted before the eleventh horn so clearly suggests (a suggestion that is confirmed in verse 24 – p.74)? However, before we look into this question it is important to check that the other four-kingdoms prophecy in the book of Daniel is consistent with the conclusions we have so far reached. That prophecy is found in Daniel 2:31-45 – a passage in which Daniel, as a young man, blindly recounts a dream that was worrying the king of Babylon, and then tells him what it means. It says the following:

> **Dan 2:31-39** [31]You looked, O king, and behold, a great statue. This statue, which was mighty, and whose brightness was excellent, stood before you; and its appearance was terrifying. [32]As for this statue, its head was of fine gold, its breast and its arms of silver, its belly and its thighs of bronze, [33]**its legs of iron, its feet partly of iron, and partly of clay**. [34]You watched until a stone was cut out [of a mountain – see v.45, p.71] without hands, which **struck the statue on its feet that were**

of iron and clay, and broke them in pieces. ³⁵Then the iron, the clay, the bronze, the silver, and the gold were broken in pieces together, and became like the chaff of the summer threshing floors. The wind carried them away, so that no place was found for them. But **the stone that struck the statue became a great mountain, and filled the whole earth.**

³⁶This is the dream; and we will tell its interpretation before the king. ³⁷You, O king, are king of kings, to whom the God of heaven has given the kingdom, the power, the strength, and the glory. ³⁸Wherever the children of men dwell, he has given the animals of the field and the birds of the sky into your hand, and has made you rule over them all. You are the head of gold. ³⁹After you, **another kingdom** will rise, **inferior** to you; and then a **third kingdom,** one of bronze, which will **rule over all the earth**…

It's worth noting at this point that the inferiority of the second kingdom in this dream does not by any means eliminate Persia as some have claimed. Although the Persian empire was far larger than Babylon's and lasted three times as long, this inferiority cannot be anything to do with size or duration. That's because it is represented by the difference between silver and gold, and the third kingdom, the one that will 'rule over *all* the earth', is represented by *bronze* (an even baser metal). Moreover, the comparatively small and short-lived Babylonian Empire is the gold. Judging from Daniel's lavish praise of his king's power and authority (v.38), we should rather expect *that* to be the yardstick (no doubt carefully chosen to allow Daniel to predict the present kingdom's demise yet still keep his head). Anyway, let's see what else the prophecy says:

Dan 2:40-45 …⁴⁰The **fourth kingdom** will be strong as iron, because iron breaks in pieces and subdues all things; and as iron that crushes all things, it will **break in pieces** and crush. ⁴¹Whereas you saw the feet and toes, partly of potters' clay, and partly of iron, **it will be a divided kingdom; but there will be**

in it the strength of the iron, because you saw the iron mixed with miry clay. [42]As the toes of the feet were part iron, and part clay, so the kingdom will be partly strong, and partly broken. [43]Whereas you saw the iron mixed with miry clay, they will mingle themselves with the seed of men; but they won't cling to one another, even as iron does not mix with clay.

[44]**In the days of those kings the God of heaven will set up a kingdom which will never be destroyed** [i.e. an eternal kingdom], nor will its sovereignty be left to another people; but it will break in pieces and consume all these kingdoms, and it will stand forever. [45]This is why you saw that **a stone was cut out of the mountain without hands**, and that it broke in pieces the iron, the bronze, the clay, the silver, and the gold; the great God has made known to the king what will happen hereafter.

Although the fourth empire in this prophecy is described as being 'divided' in its latter phase, nothing in the imagery suggests this is a four-way split (and therefore Greece). In fact, the iron and clay suggests the intermarrying is between *two types of people – strong and weak –* who won't remain united (not two *Greek dynasties*). The strong Ptolemies cannot be the clay! Surprisingly, *nowhere* in this prophecy do we see the four-way splitting typical of the Greek empire that is so evident in Daniel 8 and 11. Nevertheless, there is one comment that would definitely have identified the ***third*** empire – **the one of *bronze*** – as **Greece** in the minds of the intended readers. That is the comment that it would *'rule over all the earth'*.

By the second century BC no-one would have regarded Persia as 'ruling over all the earth'. That is because she had famously failed to subdue Greece. In the Greek world, the tales of Persia's defeats at Marathon, Salamis and Plataea by the vastly outnumbered Greek forces would have been told and retold so often that no-one could possibly have the impression that Persia ruled the whole world. In contrast, Alexander the Great was undefeated in battle and would definitely have been seen as a world-ruling king.

With the third kingdom **Greece**, the fourth must again be **Rome**. The iron legs suggest *the Republic,* and the feet hint at *future kings*.

Hence, just like Daniel 7, this passage also predicts the formation of a successful new religion (an everlasting kingdom) during the time when the Roman Empire would be ruled by kings. Since that was not the case in 165 BC, it ought to be considered another *genuine prediction* included to baffle the skeptics (though no doubt also to plant an enduring hope in those who saw themselves as the 'holy people' in the midst of their current hardships). **And yet it still came true**. It even predicts that this new religion would be formed out of Judaism. Notice how the formation of this religion is represented by 'a stone…cut out of *a mountain* without hands', and subsequently becoming '*a great mountain* filling the whole earth'. Since the second mountain obviously stands for this new religion, one can reasonably infer that the first mountain also represents a religion. And since this prophecy was written for Jews and attributed to a Jew, the only reasonable candidate for that first religion is the Jewish faith founded by Moses*. In other words, the predictions in this passage, just like those of Daniel 7 and Daniel 9, *do appear to have been exclusively fulfilled, long after their date of writing, by the rise of Christianity.*

NOTES RELATING TO CHAPTER 10

* Whilst critical scholars agree that the eternal kingdom predicted in this passage is a Jewish kingdom established by the Jewish God, they rarely tackle the issue of the two mountains. If the vision were just predicting that the Jewish faith would take over the world, why did the *first* mountain – the one from which the stone was cut – not grow to fill the whole earth? Although a stone was perhaps necessary to destroy the statue, why did the world-filling mountain come out of that stone, rather than the first mountain becoming the world-filling one? At the very least this vision is predicting the success of a *new version* of Judaism – one that would bring down those coming empires (or the beliefs that would sustain them). Yet this fact is rarely noted in critical discussions.

11. The Eleventh King of the Fourth Empire

By now you are probably thinking that something rather spooky is going on. These passages were **definitely in existence by the mid-second century BC**. There is no doubt about that. And yet, they clearly predict the takeover of the Roman Empire by a successful new religion formed out of Judaism – an event that didn't happen until **312 AD** (and needn't have happened at all). Of course, it is possible that this prophecy was *self*-fulfilling. Its very existence could have inspired people to try to bring its fulfilment about, their repeated attempts eventually proving successful. But let us now return to Daniel 7, because there is one extremely accurate prediction in this passage that simply *cannot* be accounted for in this rationalistic way. That truly astonishing flash of foresight is Daniel 7:24-25. You will find it at the end of the passage below.

> **Dan 7:19-25** [19]Then I desired to know the truth concerning the fourth animal, which was different from all of them, exceedingly terrible, whose teeth were of iron, and its claws of bronze; which devoured, broke in pieces, and stamped the residue with its feet; [20]and concerning the ten horns that were on its head, and the other horn which came up, and **before which three fell**, even that horn that had eyes, and a mouth that

spoke great things, **whose look was more stout than its fellows**.

[21]I looked, and the same horn made war with the holy people, and prevailed against them, [22]until the ancient of days came, **and judgment was given to the holy people of the Most High, and the time came when they possessed the kingdom**.

[23]Thus he said, 'The fourth animal will be a fourth kingdom on earth, which will be **different from all the kingdoms**, and will devour the whole earth, tread it down, and break it in pieces.

[24]As for the ten horns, **ten kings will arise out of this kingdom. Another will arise after them; and he will be different from the former, and he will put down three kings.** [25]**He will speak words against the Most High, and will wear out the holy people of the Most High.**

To start with, it must be made clear that these ten kings have to be the *first* ten kings to rule over the Roman Empire. If just any old ten kings were allowed, any fulfilment of this prophecy would be unsurprising. For the same reason, the king that topples three before him has to be the *eleventh* king of the Roman Empire.

But how do we define a 'king'? As a republic, Rome elected a different pair of rulers every year – rulers that were *not* regarded as kings. Moreover, in times of crisis the Roman Senate (a council of representatives of noble families) would choose a single leader and give him dictatorial powers for a short period of time (usually six months). I'm sure you'll agree with the citizens of the ancient Roman Republic that, **due to the time limits imposed upon these rulers, none of them can be considered 'kings'**.

This seems to suggest then that for someone to be considered a 'king' he must be **a ruler of a nation on whose reign there is *no specified time limit***. The first leader of the Roman Empire who was granted an unlimited reign length ought therefore to be considered the first *king* of that kingdom (regardless of whether or not he was thought of as such by his subjects or later historians).

If you agree with me on this, then you are in a position to discover the most amazing fulfilment of specific prophecy that has ever happened. The first ruler of the Roman Empire to be granted a dictatorship **with no time limit imposed** was a general called **Sulla**. In 82 BC he marched his legions on the capital to impose his will on the Senate, much as the more famous Julius Caesar was to do when he crossed the Rubicon thirty-three years later. After purging Rome of all his enemies, he resigned his dictatorship in an effort to restore the Republic – or at least to be *remembered* as a restorer of the Republic rather than the one who wrecked it. But by then, he had set a dangerous precedent. **Julius Caesar**, who just happened to be one of the citizens whom Sulla had pardoned, was the first to follow in his footsteps. After defeating all his rivals, he accepted the office of *Dictator for Life*. He was assassinated only a few weeks later on 15ᵗʰ March 44 BC (probably for that very reason).

His death was then avenged by his adopted son and heir **Octavian** (Augustus Caesar), who subsequently accomplished the very difficult task of legitimising the role of unlimited dictator (emperor) in the Roman mind – receiving life-long powers only gradually in 23 and 19 BC. However, after his death those same powers were simply inherited by each successor. First **Tiberius**, then **Caligula**, **Claudius**, **Nero**, **Galba**, **Otho**, and **Vitellius**.

That makes ten. The ten that must be matched up with the ten horns on the fourth monster's head. The eleventh horn can then only be the next Roman emperor: **Vespasian**. Considering that this horn uproots three previous ones as it grows into place, it is therefore utterly astonishing that Vespasian came to power in a year of civil war known as *'The Year of the Four Emperors'* in which **the three previous emperors, Galba, Otho and Vitellius, each got deposed and replaced in rapid succession**.

Wow! That's what I call an unexpectedly foretold occurrence! Although Vespasian is only recorded as having played a part in the downfall of Vitellius, the Jewish historian Josephus and the Roman historian Tacitus tell us certain things that suggest he probably wasn't totally uninvolved in the downfall of the other two. Captured by Vespasian (then a mere general) in Galilee, Josephus claims to have told his captor that he would become emperor, and had his life spared for doing so, *even before the death of Nero.* Moreover, on the assassination of Galba, according to Tacitus, Vespasian's brother Sabinus gained a high office in the city of Rome. This suggests he was deeply involved, and very probably working on Vespasian's behalf. And whilst Vespasian pledged his support for Otho in his war against Vitellius, in doing so he is likely to have been merely playing one of his rivals off against the other so that both would be weakened. The plan worked, as many of Otho's disgruntled supporters flocked to Vespasian's banners.

So, was this eleventh king *different from all ten of the kings that rose before him,* as verse 24 predicts? And did he '**speak against the Most High**' and '**wear out his holy people**' (which, judging from verse 21, means '*make war against them and defeat them*')?

Again the answer is an astonishing YES! Under Nero, Vespasian led the Roman army that put down the first Jewish revolt against Roman rule. As emperor, his forces **destroyed Jerusalem and her Temple**. Clearly, the term 'holy people' in the minds of the intended readers of the book of Daniel would refer to devout worshippers of the Jewish God (Daniel himself, for example), or to the Jewish nation as a whole. It is therefore intriguing to note that of those first eleven kings of the Roman Empire, *only Vespasian* fought in person against the Jews, and *only he and the Emperor Nero* who gave him that command can be regarded as *waging war* against that nation. The fact that one of these two emperors happened also to be the eleventh unlimited dictator of the Roman Empire, just as the prophecy predicts, is therefore another unexpectedly foretold occurrence. Although not as astonishing as *The Year of the Four Emperors*, or Jesus Christ's fulfilment of the most justifiable interpretation of the 'Christ' prediction in Daniel 9 (see p.39), it is still quite a remarkable coincidence.

Another intriguing fact is that, **unlike the ten kings before him, Vespasian was not the son of a senator**. Although I'm sure one could find a feature of any eleventh king that would make him distinct from his ten predecessors, this lack of legitimacy in the eyes of Rome's senators is particularly well represented by the *small size* of that eleventh horn when it first appeared (v.8, p.65).

To ensure that he was accepted by Rome's leading families, Vespasian's strategy was to distribute propaganda suggesting he was the choice of the gods. How could the nobles argue with that! He thus **justified his accession with *divine omens*, and even claimed to be the fulfilment of a *Jewish messianic prophecy***. Since the Messiah which that prophecy predicted is very likely to be the individual termed the 'Most High' in Daniel 7, we can thus be fairly confident that Vespasian did also 'speak against the Most High', as a perfect fulfilment of this prophecy requires.

And in case you are fixed upon the idea that the 'holy people' embattled by this eleventh horn have to be Christians (since it was these worshippers of the Jewish God who fulfilled the 'Eternal Kingdom' prediction in the same prophecy – see chapter 9), you may also be interested to note that Vespasian is alleged to have tried to kill all the descendants of the Jewish king David. Jesus of Nazareth was a descendent of David (or so his disciples claimed). As a result, Jesus' family – some of whom were leaders in the early Christian church of Jerusalem prior to the city's destruction – may well have suffered under that alleged bout of murderous Herod-style paranoia. They were particularly vulnerable as they were liable to protest that Jesus had already fulfilled the Messianic prophecy that Vespasian was so ruthlessly trying to lay claim to.

As far as I am concerned, I see no reason why the term 'holy people' here should not refer generally to **'devout followers of the Jewish God'** *whatever* their sectarian beliefs. I see no conflict with pious Pharisees, Sadducees and Essenes fulfilling one part of the prophecy and Christians fulfilling another. Although the content of this prophecy largely favours the Christian position (see ch.9), this shouldn't be taken as meaning that the holy people it refers to can *only* be Christians. It is worth noting, though, that since Daniel 11:32 (p.123) demonises Jews who were siding with Antiochus Epiphanes, it is quite unlikely that the writer or intended readers of the book of Daniel thought that 'holy people' referred to *all* Jews.

Whatever you may think about this relatively minor issue, it is important not to let it obscure the truly astonishing fact that this prophecy predicted that **the eleventh king of the Roman Empire would subdue three of its previous ten kings, make war on worshippers of the Jewish God, and make claims that the Jews would regard as highly blasphemous**. Although the events of 69 AD happened more than two hundred years after this prediction was written down, these events, and the first-generation senator that they brought to power, constitute a stunning and extremely visible fulfilment. The probability of such a fulfilment happening by chance is *very low indeed* – so low it is almost inconceivable!

Whilst the subduing of three previous kings need not have taken place in one year to fulfil this prophecy, the fact that it did ensured that this event was a highly memorable one that catches the eye of anyone who has read Daniel 7 and worked out its most obvious meaning. The violent removal of Galba, Otho and Vitellius – three emperors who were not related to each other, nor to the Julio-Claudian line before them, and who had no time to establish any lasting reputation – is very appropriately represented by three of the first ten horns on the fourth monster being 'plucked out by the roots' as the little eleventh horn established itself on that monster's head.

When a person who notices this looks more closely at the history of the Roman empire, she discovers that most classical historians (unlike modern scholars) regarded *Julius Caesar* as the first Roman Emperor. This naturally raises the question of what, if anything, the word 'king' in Daniel 7 should refer to in the unusual political system that Rome possessed. And when she realises that the most natural category of ruler to whom this word applies are those who have been granted *an unlimited time in office*, she very quickly discovers that there was one – and *only* one – earlier ruler who achieved that king-like status after the beginning of the Roman Republic. That was Sulla, another Caesar-like general, **which makes Vespasian indisputably *the eleventh*** (see * p.80).

And if you are inclined to quibble that Vespasian only officially subdued *Vitellius* in The Year of the Four Emperors, it's probably worth reading Tacitus' account (below) of the accession of Otho following Galba's assassination. For me, it clearly implicates Vespasian's brother Flavius Sabinus – or at least the many who in Tacitus' words 'had an eye to his brother Vespasian' – in the plot against Galba. If he were not involved, why would he be given the highest prefect post, when the only other two vacancies Tacitus mentions go to people who had either openly or secretly 'embraced the cause of Otho'? It's also worth noting that as *Prefect of the City of Rome*, in charge of all guilds and corporations and in control of the city's police force with the power to sentence people who break the emperor's laws, Sabinus had ample opportunity to steer the weak but noble Otho to his defeat by Vitellius, preparing the way for Vespasian. The fact that Vitellius didn't *remove* Sabinus all but confirms this charge. Tacitus' *Histories*, I:46 tells us:

'Everything was then ordered according to the will of the soldiery. The Praetorians chose their own prefects. One was Plotius Firmus, who had once been in the ranks, had afterwards commanded the watch, and who, while Galba was yet alive, had embraced the cause of Otho. With him was associated

Licinius Proculus, Otho's intimate friend, and consequently suspected of having encouraged his schemes. Flavius Sabinus they appointed prefect of the city, thus adopting Nero's choice, in whose reign he had held the same office, though many in choosing him had an eye to his brother Vespasian.'

That Vespasian was quite capable of engaging in such political intrigue to subdue the three contenders for the emperorship that stood in his way is supported by the Jewish historian Josephus who quotes Vespasian as saying:

"To win success by biding your time is a sounder policy than courting disaster by plunging into battle. And again, those who shine in physical combat are no more entitled to fame than those who accomplish just as much by self-discipline and brains" *(The Jewish War, IV, 366-376)*

In this way that first-generation senator who conquered the Jews succeeded in neutralising **the three senators** whose legions stood between him and the emperorship, *but only after each came to power*. He thus became **the eleventh unlimited dictator of the Roman Empire *in exact fulfilment of Daniel 7:24***. As a leader not born into Rome's ruling elite, he justified his accession with **divine omens**, including the use of a Jewish Messianic prophecy, *just as Daniel 7:25 predicts*. And in his first full year in office his forces destroyed Jerusalem and the Jewish Temple, thereby **totally vanquishing 'the holy people of the Most High'** (p.74), leaving absolutely no doubt about his fulfilment of that latter verse.

NOTES RELATING TO CHAPTER 11

* Although Rome was ruled by kings during her Monarchy Period (before 509 BC), these can be discounted on the grounds that the monster representing Rome rises after that of the Greek empire (331 BC) whose first king is considered in Daniel 8 to be Alexander the Great – the king who *first made Greece an empire*.

12. Uncertain Times

Vespasian – the eleventh unlimited dictator of the Roman Empire – is thus *extremely appropriately* represented by the little boastful eleventh horn that uproots three earlier horns on the head of the fourth monster in Daniel 7. It is almost as if this passage were written by someone living *after* 69 AD! Yet we know this cannot be so. The presence of the book of Daniel in the *Septuagint* (the surviving ancient Greek translation of the Jewish scriptures which is thought to have been completed by about 100 BC) is sufficient evidence of this – as is its very acceptance as Jewish scripture. However, you might also be interested to know that the existence of this passage in at least the first century BC is attested by the *Dead Sea Scrolls*. These include eight fragmentary copies of the book of Daniel, one of which has been carbon-dated to the late second century BC; and those copies appear to have essentially the same structure and content as the current book. Moreover, experts think that the Dead Sea Scrolls were placed in the caves at Qumran to keep them safe from Vespasian's marauding soldiers *before* 69 AD. Consequently, there is practically no chance that this accuracy could be the result of later editing. Besides, any such editor would have been inclined to make the number of those horns reflect the popular perception of Rome's history in his day (with Julius

Caesar as the first horn, and Vespasian as the *tenth*) – not the *historically accurate* view that this vision so clearly presents.

Although there are different interpretations of this passage, these tend to be forced by people who want it to predict particular things. Critical scholars, for instance, insist that the fourth beast is Greece, despite the fact that the four heads on the *third* would make everyone in 165 BC think that *it* was Greece. They do this purely so they can claim that the eleventh horn is Antiochus Epiphanes and thus avoid having to admit that the passage predicted the takeover of the Roman Empire by a Messianic sect of Judaism. Many Christian interpreters, on the other hand, bizarrely maintain that the horns – defined as 'kings' in the passage – were meant to be *'kingdoms'*. I suspect that this was mainly to exclude Jews, and later Catholics, from the 'holy people' that the prophecy refers to! Early protestant reformers, for example, became obsessed with the idea that the eleventh horn was 'the Papacy'. Others assume that it refers to some anti-Christian leader who is yet to come. They don't want it to be Vespasian because his war was against the Jews.

All these views are irrelevant for the purposes of this book because **they are not how the intended readers of the book of Daniel would have interpreted this prophecy**. If you allow yourself to interpret a prophecy any way you like, any claims you make about its fulfilment will have no statistical significance whatsoever – especially if your interpretation allows an indefinite window of time for the predicted events to take place. An anti-Christian world leader is almost bound to show up at some point in the future. So if that were what Daniel 7 predicts, the prophecy would be uninteresting. Only if you commit yourself to identifying the most *justifiable* meaning of the words and images in the passage, and only if that meaning sets the predicted events in a window of time narrow enough to make them very unlikely to occur there by chance, do you have grounds to suspect that some process other than chance is needed to explain its fulfilment. This is why we are interested in how the most probable intended readers were most likely to interpret this passage. Since that turns out to predict rare events in a narrow window of time that appear to have happened just as the prophecy says, we have a very good reason to expect that more than chance is afoot.

Those horns were *obviously* intended to stand for kings (rulers with unlimited reign-lengths). That is why Antiochus Epiphanes is represented by a horn in Daniel 8 that has some (but not all) features in common with the eleventh horn in Daniel 7. This would ensure that the intended readers interpreted that horn as a king, and they would therefore interpret the ten before it in the same way. They would thereby discover that this prophecy was one that would be unlikely to come true by chance, and was therefore worth holding onto. There are no similar arguments supporting the claim that the horns are kingdoms. Although the word translated 'kings' is used to refer to the four empires in this passage (since it probably meant 'those that rule'), it is clear from the context that these are ruling *nations*. Nothing in the context suggests that this applies to the horns on the fourth beast. In fact the actions of the eleventh suggests quite the opposite. Judging from the fact that the four-winged four-headed leopard in Daniel 7 would be identified as 'Greece' by the intended readers, kingdoms that rise out of an empire are depicted in this passage by *heads and wings*, not horns.

The horns on the fourth monster in Daniel 7 were thus definitely meant to represent kings. Moreover, the number of those horns, and **the distinctness and power of this fourth monster, and its position *after* the four-winged four-headed leopard**, make it absolutely clear that these horns were not meant to be *Greek* kings. There is no chance that the intended readers of this passage would think the four-part-divided Greek Empire was anything other than that four-winged four-headed leopard – the *third* animal in the vision. Consequently, they were sure to interpret the highly distinct and immensely powerful *fourth* animal, which broke the world up with its large iron teeth, and crushed the residue with its feet, and which had those eleven horns on its head, as the Roman Empire, which was well into its third decade of dominance over all four parts of that Greek empire when the book of Daniel was written.

Hence the eleventh horn has to have been a prediction about an eleventh king who would rise to rule over the Roman Empire long after the writer's day – a prediction that was chosen because **the intended readers would easily see that it predicted the future, thereby assuaging their suspicions about the book of Daniel's authenticity**. Nevertheless, I think these readers would have been just as amazed as I was to discover that the Roman Empire's eleventh king, Vespasian, *did indeed* fulfil the very specific claims this prophecy makes about him! Incredibly, his rise to power really did involve the toppling of three previous Roman Emperors – almost certainly via the subtle machinations of his supporters. And all three were deposed rapidly within a year, leaving no time to establish any enduring reputation, just as the uprooting of the three horns in the imagery suggests. Unlike nine of his ten predecessors, Vespasian even made war against the Jews and defeated them; and he actually spoke directly against the Most High by claiming that a prophecy of the Jewish Messiah was in fact about himself.

Intriguingly, the only feature of this prophecy that doesn't easily match an aspect of Vespasian's career is what Daniel 7 says next:

> **Dan 7:25-27** ²⁵…He will **plan to change the times and the law**; and they [the holy people] will be given into his hand until **a time, times and half a time**. ²⁶But the judgment will be set, and they will take away his dominion, to consume and to destroy it to the end. ²⁷The kingdom and the dominion, and the greatness of the kingdoms under the whole heaven, will be given to the people of the holy people of the Most High. His kingdom is an everlasting kingdom, and all dominions will serve and obey him.

No record of Vespasian planning to 'change the times and the law' (presumably the Jewish calendar and *Torah*) has come down to us. Of course, that is not to say he didn't make such plans. Like Epiphanes before him, and Hadrian six decades later, he had ample motive to take such measures, and the opportunity to enforce them. He is even reported to have spared a Jewish rabbi (Johanan Ben Zakkai) who was subsequently responsible for reinterpreting the Torah – the 'law of Moses' – to make a new temple unnecessary. And 'times' could refer to the *prophecies* Vespasian laid claim to.

However, changing times and laws is not something Vespasian is *known* for. Could that statement just be a part of this genuine prediction that *didn't* come true? After all, it hardly takes away from the stunningly accurate portrayal of Vespasian's lowly status, Jewish conquest, and rise to power. Perhaps it was even added in by the writer of the book of Daniel to make this eleventh king seem more like Antiochus Epiphanes (to get his readers to take more of an interest in this prophecy than they might otherwise do).

On the other hand, the amazing accuracy of the rest of this prediction does make one wonder whether there might be more to it than that. Another thing that adds to this suspicion is the fact that the 'little horn' representing Vespasian is later described as being 'more stout than its fellows' (p.74). What could its **sudden stoutness** prior to its fiery demise possibly represent?

To my mind, it could easily signify that this particular horn, at this stage in the dream, stands for *more than one king* – and you will notice that this is indeed what's required for a perfect portrayal of history. As we noted earlier (p.66), the beast's fiery demise symbolises the takeover of the fourth empire by *the people of the holy people of the Most High* – followers of a religion derived from Judaism, and centred on a son-of-man-like associate of the Jewish God. Since the most obvious fulfilment of this prediction is *the victory of the first Christian emperor Constantine over his rival*

Maxentius in 312 AD, that horn would need to represent **all the pagan emperors from Vespasian to Maxentius.**

Admittedly, in investigating this possibility we are assuming that there might be some process or agent that has made the imagery of this dream an accurate representation of history. But to my mind the sheer improbability that a mere guess at Rome's future would accurately predict three kings being toppled at exactly the right position in the most justifiable king-list as the famous 'Year of the Four Emperors' is ample reason to take this possibility seriously.

But what does this view entail as far as interpreting those as-yet-unmatched features of the eleventh horn is concerned? One thing it means is that the mysterious time period in verse 25 ('a time, times and half a time' – see p.84) *does not have to begin during the reign of Vespasian*. It could begin in the reign of one of those *subsequent* pagan emperors. Of course, **this would require the preposition 'He' in verse 25 to have been inserted by a later editor in place of 'A successor'**. But given that this prophecy was intended to resemble those of Antiochus, I don't think that is too implausible. The time period – 'a time, times and half a time' – would thus be the length of a time of persecution when the 'holy people' would be 'given into the hand' of those pagan rulers; and it must end shortly before Constantine's victory in 312 AD (see verse 22, p.74). Moreover, we know that the 'holy people' must include both Jews and Christians – in other words, all worshippers of the Jewish God. Jews must be included because Daniel was a Jew and Jews were the intended readers of this prophecy; and Christians because Christianity fulfils the prophecy's 'Eternal Kingdom' prediction.

With these assumptions there is only one historical event that could possibly mark the *end* of that time period: the *Edict of Toleration* issued by the emperor Galerius in the spring of 311 that officially ended the *Great Persecution* – the last and most severe Roman suppression of Christianity. Hence, if our supposition is true we ought to find an equally salient historical event, that is easily seen to be the beginning of a time of persecution with this end-point, *at exactly the length of the time period before it*. All we now need to do is identify what that time period is most likely to mean.

Most interpreters assume the 'times' are 'years', making the 'time, times and half a time' *three-and-a-half years* long; and this view is clearly supported by Daniel 12:11, where the writer of the book of Daniel interprets 'a time, times and a half' as '1290 *days*' (see p.124). It is also supported by Daniel 4:16, 23, 25 and 32, where King Nebuchadnezzar's illness is to last 'seven *times*'. However, there is good reason to suspect that this was not what the *original* author intended. For a start, the writer of Daniel 12 has his hero express total bewilderment on hearing this time phrase, which probably means he didn't understand it himself. He may thus have made it mean 'years' simply to predict the imminent intervention of God his readers were yearning for. And the easiest way for him to do that was by changing 'years' to 'times' in Daniel 4.

It is also worth considering that if the time of persecution predicted in Daniel 7 were intended to be three-and-a-half years long, one would expect the prophecy to say 'half a seven' (or at least use the usual word for year). But the strongest reason to doubt that those 'times' were meant to be years is that **a mere three-and-a-half years is hardly a very respectable duration for a time of hardship in ancient Jewish history**. After all, they had to wander the desert for *forty* years, were exiles in Babylon for at least *forty-seven*, and slaves in Egypt for longer still.

So what else could those times have meant? To my mind the only other reasonable possibility is that, like the 'sevens' in Daniel 9, they stood for the length of a cycle that the Jews were supposed to keep as part of their sacred law of Moses. Aside from those 'sevens' and the usual seven-day weeks, there appears to be only one other such cycle: The fifty-year *Jubilee period* of Leviticus

25:8-10 (p.46*) the source of the 'sevens' in Daniel 9. Hence 'fifty years' is the best meaning for 'time' in Daniel 7, making the 'time, times and half a time' add up to a full *175* **years** (50 + 100 + 25).

It is therefore astonishing that exactly 175 years before the spring of 311 AD was the spring of 136 AD, the very time Hadrian finished off the last vestiges of Jewish resistance in Judea before chasing the Jews out of their traditional homeland. For the next 175 years none of the holy people (neither Jews nor Christians) had any state protection. **They were indeed 'given into the hand' of those pagan kings for exactly 'a time, times and half a time'.**

NOTES RELATING TO CHAPTER 12

* For practical reasons the Jews appear to have interpreted this requirement as a 49-year cycle. They made the 'fiftieth year' – when the planting of crops was forbidden (just as it was every Sabbath year) – the first year of the next cycle. That way the Sabbath and Jubilee cycles would not get out of step, and by starting each set of seven years with a Sabbath year they could avoid having two consecutive years when crops weren't to be planted. However, the Sabbath year is clearly meant to be the *seventh* of each seven in Leviticus 25:8-10 (p.46); and if so, they could only keep both that rule and the 'six years of planting' law in Lev. 25:3 (p.10) by starting the next Sabbath cycle *after* the Jubilee year. Hence, it seems to me that the literal meaning of the Jubilee cycle in Lev. 25:10 – and therefore each of Daniel's 'times' – is '*50* years', not 49. Of course, due to the way this passage was traditionally interpreted, '49 years' cannot be discounted, which does affect our assessment of how improbable the observed fulfilment is. If the 'times' were interpreted as 49-year periods, the 'time, times and half a time' (going backwards from 311) would bring us to a year or so after Hadrian's death, by which time the 'holy people' had already been given into the hand of those pagan emperors for more than three years. It is important to notice that due to the very few historical events that could constitute this handing-over point, the fact that we thus have two justifiable possibilities for the time period (thereby doubling the probability of a chance fulfilment) *still does not make such a fulfilment particularly likely!* (For more on this see the note on p.93).

13. The Mouth and The Eyes

With the stoutness of the eleventh horn interpreted as a *sequence* of kings, we have found that the most justifiable meaning of 'a time, times and half a time' *perfectly spans the interval over which the 'holy people' were stateless victims of Roman oppression.* However, this interpretation would not have been obvious to the intended readers of this passage, making it hard to argue that its fulfilment was an unexpectedly *foretold* occurrence. Unlike us, they had no idea how many pagan Roman rulers there'd be before 'the people of the holy people of the Most High' took over. So is there anything in the prophecy or elsewhere in Daniel that ought to have made them think it predicted more than eleven pagan kings?

One possibility is the horns in Daniel 8 (p.121). Most of the long horns in that passage do signify successions of kings. However, their length variations are ambiguous. Those of the ram's horns may signify different numbers of rulers, but could also represent the dominance of the Persians over the Medes. The lengths of the first and last horn of the goat, on the other hand, almost certainly represent the arrogance of *individual* powerful kings (the first being Alexander the Great, and the last, Antiochus Epiphanes). Hence Daniel 8 would have been unhelpful in this regard.

As far as I can see, there is only one thing that could have pointed those readers to this view of the eleventh horn's later stoutness, and that is the phrase 'a time, times and half a time'. As we saw in chapter 12, this time phrase is only reasonably interpreted as 175 years (or 171.5 years if the 'times' are taken to be 49 rather than 50 years long) – much longer than the lifetime of any single king.

To see that, though, they would have had to recognise that Daniel 11-12 was likely to be a forgery. That is because, to add a sense of urgency and imminent hope to his "predicted" resistance of the faithful against their Seleucid oppressors – which was of course taking place at the time of writing – the writer of Daniel 12:11 interprets the phrase 'a time, times, and a half' as 1290 days (see Appendix p.124): In other words, around *three-and-a-half years*. Hence, in order to arrive at our more-justifiable view of that time period, his readers would have had to ignore this passage, yet still believe in Daniel 7 (which they were obviously unlikely to do).

Due to the presence of Daniel 12:11, any early reader of the book of Daniel was likely to think that Daniel 7 predicted the takeover of the Roman Empire by Jews (or Christians) only *three-and-a-half years* or so after those 'holy people' were 'given into the hand of' the eleventh king of that empire (a king who would replace three previous Roman Emperors). Amazingly, they did indeed get given into the hand of that king (Vespasian), though those who hadn't joined the rebellion of 66-74 AD did get to keep their land and some limited form of self-government afterwards. And even more amazingly, that king did also rise to power with the rapid overthrow of three previous kings, just as the prophecy predicted. In view of this, learned Jews at the time of Vespasian, such as the historian Josephus, may well have been expecting a takeover of the Roman Empire by their defeated kindred three-and-a-half years or so after the fall of Jerusalem in 70 AD, or Masada in 74. They would have been bitterly disappointed when that failed to occur despite the initially promising signs of this prophecy's accuracy.

Now, assuming for a moment that the book of Daniel was the work of a God, did that God make a mistake in leaving Daniel 12:11 as it stands? To see the answer to this question, consider what might have transpired had Daniel 12:11 said '175 years' or any other decades-long time period. The specificity of such a prediction would undoubtedly have become known to the Romans, and that would almost certainly have resulted in an exponential increase in the sufferings of the holy people as their oppressors sought to thwart any possibility of this prediction coming true. Only if they were likely to interpret the 'time, times and half a time' as a relatively short time period could such increased suffering be avoided. The fall of Jerusalem, and the inevitable enslavement and taxation that followed, would already be thought sufficient to prevent that predicted takeover. And after the time period had elapsed, everyone would just assume the prophecy had failed. Hence, to ensure the survival of his people, it would be in God's interests to leave that writer's interpretation alone. Perhaps that is what Jesus Christ was alluding to in Matthew 24:22 when, after predicting that same persecution, he says, 'but for the sake of the chosen ones, those days will be shortened' (p.46). Judging from the non-calendrical meaning of 'seven' needed to make Daniel 9 perfectly predict the Triumphal Entry of Christ, if the fulfilment of these prophecies is the work of a God, that God never meant them to be used to work out the timing of something *in advance*. Their accuracy can only have been intended as a sign for later scholars.

Realising the suspicious nature of Daniel 11-12, those scholars can confidently reject the interpretation of 'a time, times and half a time' which the writer of that passage made up for propaganda purposes. Like me, they will rightly wonder why his hero doesn't answer the hovering, fiery-eyed demigod who gives him this interpretation in Daniel 12:11, with the words "Oh I see! Why didn't you just say 'a year, two years, and half a year'? Having rejected that nonsensical interpretation, they will then be drawn to Jewish scripture to see if there are any other obvious units of time that have not been labelled elsewhere in Daniel. They would soon realise that the only other option is the fifty-year (or forty-nine-year) *Jubilee* period (p.46). Knowing that Christianity was the sect of Judaism that took over the Roman Empire in a perfect fulfilment of Daniel 7:14-18 (p.67) and Daniel 2:35 & 44-45 (p.69-71), they would then note that the official end of the last persecution of Christians by the pagan Roman emperors was Galerius' *Edict of Toleration* in the spring of 311. To identify the most reasonable starting point for the time of persecution that Daniel 7:25 alludes to (the one based upon the literal 50-year 'times' – see * p.93), they would consequently count back 175 years from that date. And they would thereby immediately discover that they were in the spring of 136 AD – the very time Hadrian's soldiers brutally finished off the remaining pockets of resistance in Judea before banning the holy people from Jerusalem, and depopulating their ravaged homeland.

Although you might think there'd be other events that this 'handing over' point could constitute, there are in fact very few. In subsequent Jewish history there is no similarly disastrous clash with Rome; and save for the Kitos war of 115-7, the same applies from 75 AD until the Jews started losing to Hadrian in 134. Hence you must admit that the ending of Bar Kokhba's revolt is by far the most *suitable* of the very few historical events that could reasonably be described as the holy people being 'given into the hand' of the Roman Emperors. From that time on, the Jews could no longer offer armed resistance to Rome's antisemitic demands. And until 'judgement was given to them' in the form of the 311 AD *Edict of Toleration*, the Christians suffered a similar state of frequent persecution. Moreover, Hadrian's well-known attempt to change the Jewish calendar, and outlaw circumcision, would then fit neatly with the mention of an attempt to 'change the times and the law' which precedes this disastrous handing-over in verse 25 (p.84).

Realising this, it is rather fascinating that the eleventh horn in the imagery not only becomes stouter than all the others, but gains a mouth and eyes. The boastful mouth is, of course, a fitting symbol for Vespasian, who justified his accession with divine omens (p.77), and a claim to be the fulfilment of a Jewish prophecy. Consequently, the eyes ought to represent *Hadrian*, the Roman emperor into whose hands the holy people were first given.

The fascinating thing is that Hadrian was an emperor best known for seeing. Unlike the other emperors, he constantly toured his vast empire to see its territories with his own eyes. Eyes are thus an *extremely appropriate* symbol for that particular emperor.

As we have now seen, this passage contains an astoundingly perfect representation of the timing of major historical events and the character of their participants. This strongly suggests to me that its fulfilment was no mere coincidence. Nevertheless, hindsight isn't an option. And as we shall see in the next chapter, the nature of the historical events that it predicts appears to rule out self-fulfilment too. Something very strange must be going on here.

NOTES RELATING TO CHAPTER 13

* Admittedly, in claiming that there are only two reasonable starting points for the 'time, times and half a time', I have assumed that the years implicit in those 'times' have to be *normal calendar* years (in other words, *approximate solar* years). I think this is justified because of the use of the word 'times' rather than 'fifties'. Had the latter been used, we would need to calculate the time period using the 360-day years suggested by the numbers of days in Daniel 12:11. However, the word 'times' merely suggests the length of a time interval (of religious significance). Hence its meaning is most probably the length of the time interval indicated by Leviticus 25:10 (fifty or forty-nine *calendar* years).

On the other hand, the fact that there are three *potential* meanings for the word 'year' implicit in that time period (just as there were for the 'sevens' in Daniel 9) does mean that there are actually six – not two – *possible* starting points for this time period. All six would have to be taken into account when assessing the probability that this prophecy was fulfilled by chance. However, it is worth noting that none of the other five potential starting points coincides with a historical event that fulfils the prediction, 'the holy people will be *given into his hand* for 175 [or 171.5] years' (where 'his' refers to one of the pagan successors of Vespasian – see p.86). As I have said, there are very few historical events that could possibly fit this description (especially in view of the length of the time of persecution that they must begin). The fact that our extremely justifiable interpretation of the time period picks out the event that fits this description *best*, is therefore another extraordinary observation about this prophecy.

Amazingly, that event is also implicit in the prophecy of Daniel 9:26-27 that we met in chapter 6. It comes only a year or so after Hadrian's ending of sacrifice through the victories of his general Severus in 135. And it constitutes the point when the last Jewish resistance stopped and the persecution began in earnest. That it picks out an event so central to that which fulfils another prophecy in the same book is remarkable. It is almost as if Daniel 9 was an "explanation" of the events predicted by the dream in Daniel 7 – which is exactly what the mysterious phrase 'and will have nothing' suggests it was. As I speculated in the notes at the end of chapter 4 (p.34), the phrase 'and will have nothing' in Daniel 9:26 would make sense if the prophecy in Daniel 9 were once part of an epilogue to the *Aramaic* book of Daniel (chapters 2-7). That prophecy could then be telling Daniel that the 'Most High' (rendered 'Most Holy' by the Hebrew translator) is to be a Christ who would arrive at Jerusalem at a specific time, and get put to death *having none of the glory and power Daniel 7 predicts*. Subsequently, Jerusalem and the Temple will get destroyed (by the mouth of the eleventh horn in Daniel 7), and then a king of the same people (the eyes of that horn) will end the sacrifice and offering at another specified time and raise an abomination on an infamous overspreading. Maybe that original Daniel 9 even ended with the words of Daniel 12:7 (p.124): *"It will be for a time, times and a half; and when they have finished breaking in pieces the power of the holy people, all these things will be finished"*, thus completing its explanation of Daniel 7. Using this very conclusion, the later Hebrew editor wrote Daniel 12:7; and, not wanting too much repetition, left it out of his translation of Daniel 9. And lest you think this speculation baseless, consider this: Christ *himself* (p.46) uses the words of Daniel 12:1 (and 9:27) in his prophecy of *this* persecution!

14. Explaining the Accuracy

Due to the rare, time-limited and momentous nature of the events predicted by Daniel 2, 7 and 9 (when interpreted in the most justifiable way the intended readers of Daniel could interpret them), their perfect fulfilment is solid evidence of the involvement of some superhuman intelligence in the course of history. As scholars have rightly observed, the content of Daniel 8 and 11 fixes their date of completion to before 160 BC (a date consistent with the relevant archaeological and textual evidence). What scholars don't tell you is that, based upon the perception of history in Daniel 8 and 11, it is very likely that Daniel 2, 7 and 9 were chosen for the book of Daniel precisely because its intended readers would interpret them – for very obvious reasons – as predictions of the distant future. The critical consensus is flawed because it fails to take account of the fact that a writer trying to pass off the book of Daniel as the work of an ancient prophet had every reason to include such genuine predictions within it (and would be very likely to choose ones that bore some resemblance to recent events).

Regardless of how critical scholars try to account for their content, what we can say for certain is that the most justifiable interpretation of each of these passages *does predict the future well beyond 160 BC.* And in each case, the prediction it makes has proven stunningly accurate. Moreover, due to the nature of the events that fulfilled these predictions, it is not possible to realistically argue that they were *self*-fulfilled. Hadrian would never have chosen to die seven years after founding Aelia Capitolina; Vespasian had no control over the number of kings he had to topple to get to power; and Jesus (without God) probably couldn't have worked how long 69 'sevens' was in normal calendar years.

Consequently, the only *rational* explanation for their astonishing accuracy isn't chance. It is the view that some intelligent entity with superhuman powers and longevity has influenced people during subsequent history to ensure that those events took place.

Is that really a rational possibility? If you are not a religious person you might be thinking definitely not. But before you completely rule it out, ask yourself what you yourself actually are. I don't mean what you *as a human organism* are, but you as in the *consciousness* (the stream of experiences) somewhere in the brain of that organism. Within that stream of experiences all the outputs of its various sensory systems are combined into a holistic representation. You feel as though you *are* that organism. But you are really something far, far smaller; something buried deep inside its brain. We don't know for sure what that something is yet. But judging from our scientific explanations of other biologically organised entities, we should be fairly confident that it affects the brain in a way that's dependent upon its experiences. Moreover, we have every reason to expect it to be some sort of *ordinary matter* that the brain has utilised for a purpose, and not something complex or supernatural that only brains or organisms can produce.

If ordinary matter can thus consist of experiences and affect surrounding matter on the basis of these experiences, and if it has within it the capacity for a sense of agency (as we appear to), who's to say the universe itself doesn't automatically have those capacities? Indeed, in his 1928 book *The Nature of the Physical World* the famous astrophysicist Sir Arthur Eddington reached the conclusion that it must have. Obviously any experience we might thus grant the universe couldn't evolve to have an intelligent, comprehensible form via natural selection because it isn't a biological entity. However, it is possible that it wouldn't need to. Ours only needed to evolve because it had to represent things that are *outside it* – things like visual images, bodily feelings, auditory vibrations, temperature gradients, etc. With the universe, its experiences would automatically represent the matter they constitute. If it could manipulate them (and had an in-built drive to do so), then provided it constantly remembered what had gone before, it could automatically be an intelligent creative being *without needing a brain or any other biological paraphernalia.*

As a philosopher who has studied the mind for decades, I am confident that such a being is not only possible, but very likely to exist. If so, is it reasonable to *doubt* that it would take an interest in humanity? After all, as far as we are currently aware, what's been happening on the surface of planet earth over the last few thousand years is by far the most unusual and interesting thing taking place in the whole universe. Should we not *expect* such a being to take an interest in entities controlled by consciousnesses like itself who are able to manipulate their environment in a creative way and generate the marvels of art and technology that we see around us?

Now, it may be that you have no problem believing in a God who would take an interest in human affairs. But you might still be wondering why I have suggested that such accurate prophecies would require God to *act through history.* Couldn't God just 'look into the future' and *tell* his prophet Daniel what was to happen?

Whilst I'm quite reluctant to speculate on what God can and cannot do, I think such an ability poses insurmountable logical problems – especially if we have a form of free will, as I believe we do. If that is the case, the future is essentially undecided, so what is there for this God to see? Hence, I think such accurate prophecies come about because God first inspires them, or becomes aware of their existence, and then acts over the intervening time period to ensure that the events they predict come to pass. Judging from the way Christ deliberately acted to fulfil ancient prophecies in the gospel accounts (Matthew 21:1-5), this clearly appears to be what the early Christian writers thought too.

Another concern that readers might have with this proposal is the fact that this objective evidence of the influence of a God appears to be only evident in the book of Daniel. Of all the other books of prophecy in the Old Testament and elsewhere, none of them has anything like the combination of specific predictions and datable context that we find in the book of Daniel. As St Jerome noted in his early-fifth-century *Commentary on Daniel* (Jerome, p.15),

> 'None of the prophets has so clearly spoken concerning Christ as has this prophet Daniel. For not only did he assert that He would come, a prediction common to the other prophets as well, but also he set forth the very time at which He would come. Moreover, he went through the various kings in order, stated the actual number of years involved, and announced beforehand the clearest signs of events to come.'

If such a being wanted us to recognise 'his' presence, wouldn't he leave us a lot *more* objective evidence to base our faith on than three hotly contested passages in an Old Testament book of clearly questionable authenticity?

If that God is the Christian God (as the content of those fulfilled prophecies suggests), I suspect the answer to this question is *probably not*. The reason is *not* that this God doesn't want us to have this faith. According to the New Testament writers, he very much does. It is that he wants to give us the evidence we need directly and personally when we ask for it, rather than through interfering in a lot of other human lives. It would have been no trivial task to ensure the occurrence of a *Year of the Four Emperors* at just the right time in history to fulfil Daniel 7 (especially given the strong republican tradition of the Romans). God would have had to ensure that the all-too-regular conflicts between nations in the ancient world had suitable outcomes. For there to be any point in fulfilling these prophecies, he'd also have had to ensure the survival of the book of Daniel for many centuries when the only copying machines available were human beings. And to guarantee the fulfilment of Daniel 9, he'd even have had to keep Hadrian alive until exactly seven years after the founding of Aelia Capitolina (see chapter 7). Yet had he chosen instead to fulfil predictions of events that were *less* momentous, or at the other extreme seemingly *miraculous*, the fulfilment would be vulnerable to the claim that it was either orchestrated or invented by humans. Hence I think God is only doing what's needed to get our attention.

But why would God even go to that much trouble if he could just speak to us directly as he presumably did to the writer of Daniel 2, Daniel 7 and Daniel 9:24-27? Perhaps it is because doing that would mean interfering uninvited in *everybody's* life. Although to produce this objective evidence of his existence requires him to influence a lot of human decisions, that would be nothing compared to the number of human beings he'd be influencing uninvited if he revealed himself to everyone *directly*. The Christian God is not in the business of this. He wants people to learn of his existence indirectly through other people and the wonders of creation, and then invite him into their lives. After that he is apparently very willing to reveal himself directly to individuals.

Hence, to my mind, if God really did ensure the fulfilment of these prophecies, as all the evidence strongly suggests, he did so to provide the sort of evidence that would allow scientific people who genuinely seek the most reasonable explanations for things to take his existence seriously as a potential explanation for a set of facts that cannot be accounted for in any more-justifiable way. Only that sort of evidence will give such people a reason to contemplate the possibility of the Christian God's existence, and thereby the opportunity to invite that God to reveal himself directly to them.

Daniel 2, 7 and 9 could thus be like the nail-marks in Jesus' hands and the spear-hole in his side that he showed his disciple Thomas who was doubting his resurrection. Those wounds were objective evidence for Thomas – evidence that he was invited to examine with his hands in the practical way of a scientist – so that, despite his skeptical nature, he could still believe that Jesus was from God, and hence follow his instruction to invite that God into his life. The accuracy and content of Daniel 2, 7 and 9 convinces me that they serve the same function for skeptical people today. Provided those people are willing to look rationally at the evidence, and ask themselves what is the most *reasonable* interpretation of those prophecies, and provided they are prepared to look *critically* at what the experts have said about them, and study the relevant history when they discover that by chance or design these prophecies *definitely did predict the future*, they will be inexorably led to the view that perhaps the Christian God does exist after all.

One final point I'd like to make in this chapter is that nothing requires God to have inspired the prophecies he chooses to make use of. This book identifies Daniel 8 and Daniel 11 as forgeries (or what scholars often call 'pseudonymous' or 'pseudepigraphic'). However, their content is so pivotal in defending the claim that Daniel 2, 7 and 9 are genuine that I'm sure their inclusion was no accident. The book of Daniel seems far too important for that.

Reach here your finger, and see my hands.
Reach here your hand, and put it into my side.
Don't be unbelieving, but believe!

John 20:27

15. Against the Porphyrians

We have now almost finished our analysis of the content of the book of Daniel. However, I'd like to put the conclusions we've reached so far into a historical perspective before presenting my final piece of evidence against the current mainstream position. The book of Daniel contains such strong objective evidence of the work of the Christian God that it was singled out by classical philosophers trying to curb the rapid growth of Christianity in the second and third centuries AD. One of these was the Greek philosopher Porphyry, who analysed Daniel in the twelfth book of his fifteen-volume polemic *Against the Christians* – a work that survives only in the words of Christian intellectuals like St Jerome who responded to Porphyry's challenge. What Jerome and those other Christian apologists did not take seriously enough is the fact that Porphyry appears to have been right about Daniel 8 and Daniel 11. As far as we know, he was the first to claim that these passages were written from hindsight – a claim that is strongly supported by their content and varying accuracy. However, like critical scholars today, he also argued that Daniel 7 was about Antiochus Epiphanes. As we saw in chapter 8, the content of that passage – and the purpose of the book of Daniel that Porphyry's position implies – does not support this view. In fact, it blatantly contradicts it. The content of Daniel 7, and the historical context in which Porphyry believed the book was written, makes his account of that chapter so unlikely to be what the intended readers would think that it begs the question of what motivated Porphyry to propose it.

It is interesting to note that, unlike most modern critical scholars, Porphyry didn't actually question the extremely justifiable conclusions that we reached in chapter 8 concerning the *first three* beasts in Daniel 7 – conclusions that were reached for similar reasons by everyone who commented on Daniel prior to Porphyry's time and for many centuries afterwards. He readily accepted that the *four-headed, four-winged leopard* in that dream was Alexander's *four-part-divided Greek empire*, and the bear with **a raised and lowered side**, the Medo-Persian Empire that Alexander conquered (the same empire represented by the ram in Daniel 8 that has **one horn higher than the other**). Instead, he merely argued that the fourth monster was not the Roman Empire, but the *divided phase* of the Greek Empire, and in particular the Greek *Seleucid kingdom* from which Antiochus Epiphanes arose.

You can probably see why this view isn't widely held today. If the intended readers of Daniel had already interpreted the four heads and four wings of the *Leopard* as those four Greek kingdoms, they were hardly going to expect these kingdoms to be represented a second time in the dream – and certainly not in the form of the highly distinct fourth monster standing for a kingdom that would be 'different from all the kingdoms' (v.23, p.74). For that fourth empire to be different from all the previous empires, it could not possibly be a *successor kingdom* – like the Seleucid and Ptolemaic empires that Porphyry identifies it as – a kingdom that emerged from one of those previous empires and whose rulers belonged to the same nation and saw themselves as the legitimate successors of the founder of that third empire. As if that weren't conclusive enough, the immense strength of the fourth empire makes this view clearly inconsistent with the claim in Daniel 8:22 that the divided phase of the Greek empire would be *weaker* than its united phase – see Appendix p.122 (a claim that is repeated in Daniel 11:4, p.10).

But however much Porphyry may be criticised for this view, it is no worse than the views of mainstream critical scholars today. At least Porphyry's view does not demand that the intended readers interpret the four-headed, four-winged leopard as *Persia*, in complete denial of the compiler's perception of history presented so clearly for them to read in Daniel 8 and Daniel 11. As we have seen, the problem with the claims of Porphyry and subsequent critical scholars is that they don't take into account the fact that the writer of Daniel 11 and Daniel 8 had an extremely good reason to include *predictions of the distant future* in this book. He even had reason to predict distant future events that bore some resemblance to the main events of Daniel 8 and Daniel 11 (since reminders of recent history within his unmistakably genuine predictions of the future would interest his readers in those genuine predictions, and make the inclusion of Daniel 8 and 11 in this supposedly ancient book seem a bit more plausible). **Without such predictions, his work was likely to be dismissed as a forgery**. Since the Roman Empire was already dominant in his day, any prophecy in Daniel that appears to be making a prediction about the future of that empire was therefore probably included for exactly this purpose.

Porphyry was, of course, writing *Against the Christians*. That might explain why he has excluded this far-more-plausible explanation for the dream's content. Modern critical scholars, on the other hand, would no doubt claim no such bias. Are we really supposed to believe that they have not *thought* of this extremely plausible scenario? Or are they perhaps not as impartial as they ought to be due to their desire to avoid the stigma of being labelled 'conservative'? This is no trivial matter. The facts we have uncovered indicate that Daniel 2, 7 and 9 are scientific evidence of a *very real God*. Denying them the scholarly attention they deserve puts this amazing discovery out-of-reach for the average taxpayer.

Daniel also wrote concerning the Roman government,
and that our country should be made desolate by them…

Flavius Josephus (Antiquities of the Jews, Book X, 11:7)

Judas chose Eupolemus the son of John, the son of Accos,
and Jason the son of Eleazar, and sent them to Rome,
to establish friendship and alliance with them,
and that they should take the yoke from them;
for they saw that the kingdom of the Greeks
did keep Israel in bondage.
And they went to Rome (and the way was exceedingly long),
and they entered into the senate house, and answered and said,
Judas, who is also called Maccabaeus, and his kindred,
and the people of the Jews, have sent us to you,
to make a confederacy and peace with you,
and that we might be registered your confederates and friends.

1 Maccabees 8:17-20 (The Jewish Embassy to Rome in 161 BC)

16. EP-GP or GP-EP and the Absence of 'Rome'

We have throughout this book assumed that the book of Daniel was compiled carefully in an unhurried manner. Its compiler (around 165 BC) had time, not only to write his carefully crafted *ex eventu* prophecies of Antiochus Epiphanes, but also to search through a bank of ancient predictions, work out what his readers would most probably understand them to mean, and then choose those that predicted distant future events that bore similarities to recent ones. I call this the *EP-GP* scenario (*Ex eventu Prophecy* calls for *Genuine Predictions*).

There is, however, another possibility. What if the compiler was in a hurry? What if he had no time to look for suitable ancient prophecies, and instead happened to have a pile of scrolls that contained essentially the material we find in the Aramaic section of the current book (Daniel 2-7) together with the Seventy 'Sevens' prophecy of Daniel 9?

As far as I can see, it is possible that he might one day have glanced through that material, noticed Daniel 7 and Daniel 9 and, without stopping to think about what these prophecies actually predicted, thought "Wow! That might be a prophecy of Antiochus

Epiphanes!" (much as mainstream critical scholars do today). Wanting to inspire resilience in his suffering comrades, he quickly put the Aramaic part of the book of Daniel together... and then had second thoughts. He began to worry about whether or not these two prophecies really did predict Epiphanes. If they didn't, circulating this book could prove counterproductive – demoralising the faithful with the thought that God didn't really care about their current troubles. But remember, he had no time to check out the details. Instead, he thought to himself, "I'll just create a couple of prophecies in a similar style (Daniel 8 and Daniel 11) that actually *do* predict Antiochus Epiphanes, and add them to the book!".

That's the *GP-EP* scenario. As you can see, it is a lot closer to the current views of critical scholars. The main difference is that in this scenario Daniel 7 and Daniel 9 were not *created* with Antiochus Epiphanes in mind. The compiler may have selected these prophecies because at first glance the king they depicted seemed a bit like Antiochus Epiphanes, but he did not write them or edit them to make them predict Epiphanes, and neither did their original author. How do we know? Because as we have seen throughout this book, they *don't* predict Antiochus Epiphanes, and would not have seemed as though they did to anyone at the time who read them carefully. This is why their meaning must be defined as what the *intended reader* in 165 BC would think (rather than what the compiler may or may not have thought).

Of course, you might be wondering why such a writer wouldn't just alter these ancient prophecies to *make* them predict Antiochus Epiphanes. Why write new prophecies when you could just doctor the old ones a bit? But there are plausible reasons why he might not *want* to change those ancient prophecies. One is obviously the EP-GP reason – the fact that if he was going to include *ex eventu* prophecies of Epiphanes in his book, it would also need *genuine predictions of the future* to counter suspicions that it was a forgery. As we have seen, Daniel 7 and Daniel 9 are ideal for this purpose.

Another possible reason is that these prophecies may have been in existence for a very long time before his day. If that were the case, other people may have copies of them. If his book came out containing a prophecy that was almost identical to one that these people owned – just edited a little to make it predict Epiphanes – the owners of those other versions of the prophecy were bound to notice and denounce the book of Daniel as a forgery. Their treasured manuscripts would be even stronger evidence of forgery than the relatively detailed but hitherto unheard-of predictions of Epiphanes' recent actions that the compiler of the book of Daniel almost certainly wrote himself in Daniel 8 and Daniel 11.

The possibility that other people might have copies of the prophecies now found in Daniel 2, Daniel 7 and Daniel 9 might also explain why these prophecies were not simply left out when the writer realised they didn't predict Epiphanes at all. If they were already associated with the tales found in the Aramaic part of the book of Daniel, replacing them entirely with his Hebrew prophecies would also raise suspicions. It would be far more risky than just proclaiming the discovery of a couple of new scrolls that this little-known collaborator with the Babylonian regime had sealed up until 'the time of the end'.

As you can see, the *Genuine Prediction calls for Ex eventu Prophecy* (GP-EP) scenario can be defended, and may be more appealing to critical scholars due to the fact that it allows the compiler's first impression of these prophecies to preserve some elements of the current critical consensus. Nevertheless, it doesn't take away from the fact that a careful Jewish reader of the book of Daniel in 165 BC was never going to interpret these prophecies as anything but predictions of the future – so this *must* have been what they were.

The insertion of Daniel 8 right after Daniel 7, and a prayer derived from the book of Nehemiah directly in front of the *Seventy*

'Sevens' prophecy in Daniel 9, is extremely strong evidence that the compiler definitely wanted his readers to recognise this fact. The likely origin of the prayer in Daniel 9 – and even its simple resemblance to Nehemiah's prayer that the compiler could hardly have missed – **clearly indicates that Nehemiah's permission to rebuild Jerusalem was what he believed the starting point of the 483-year time period in Daniel 9 to be**. And as we saw in the eighth chapter of this book, the features of the two beasts in Daniel 8 (the asymmetry of the ram's two horns and the quadruple nature of the goat's) are a very close analogy to those of the *middle* two beasts in Daniel 7. This makes it unreasonable to argue that the compiler did not think the asymmetrically-sided bear and four-headed leopard in Daniel 7 stood for the Medo-Persian and Greek empires respectively. Moreover, the vivid description of the power and distinctness of the fourth monster in Daniel 7, together with its iron teeth and tendency to break its victims into pieces, make it extremely unlikely that the relatively well-informed writer of Daniel 11 would think it was anything other than the Roman empire – the empire that had recently broken up Macedon.

Although the dominance of Rome is only alluded to a couple of times in Daniel 11, it is a big step to conclude from this that such a well-informed writer was completely unaware of a major political reality that had come into being *more than twenty years before he wrote this passage*. Rome isn't specifically mentioned in Daniel 11 because Daniel 11 was intended to predict Epiphanes. There was no need to bring Rome into it. Rome had at that time played no significant part in Jewish affairs, so we should not expect her to feature much in this writer's *ex eventu* prophecies. Nevertheless, this writer does mention Greece and Persia by name in both Daniel 11 and Daniel 8. So one might legitimately wonder why he only refers to Rome indirectly in Daniel 11 as 'a commander' (Daniel 11:18) and 'Kittim' (Daniel 11:30) – a generic term often translated 'Western Coastlands', which at the time seems to have referred to coastlands west of what is now Turkey, not just Italy.

In actual fact, not mentioning Rome by name might actually be the strongest evidence we have of the compiler's *awareness* of Rome's dominance. To have the opportunity, literacy skills and sources needed to write and promote the book of Daniel, that compiler would have to be a learned Jewish priest or aristocrat – one of the leading men in Jewish society. As such, he would at that time have known that Rome constituted a powerful potential ally in their fight against Seleucid control. After all, the Jews sent an embassy to the Senate only a few years after the book of Daniel was written. Due to the fact that Daniel 7 and Daniel 2 clearly predict the take-over of the Roman Empire by followers of Daniel's God, if the writer of the book of Daniel were to mention Rome by name anywhere in that book, he could completely scupper any chance they had of forming such a powerful alliance. Of course, the very inclusion of these prophecies was a risk. However, at least the absence of any explicit identification of the fourth empire allowed the possibility of *plausible deniability* should the issue come up in future negotiations. The negotiators could claim it was Parthia, for example, the rising power in the east, and Rome's later enemy. Less convincingly, they could try to argue that it was the Seleucid Empire as critical scholars do today. (Incidentally, this important consideration might also explain why Daniel doesn't *recognise* the fourth monster in Daniel 7. And as with so many other obvious possibilities discussed in this book, it is not something that critical scholars appear to have given much thought to).

Finally, it's worth noting that my GP-EP account of Daniel 8 – that it was inserted to highlight Daniel 7, and to ensure that the intended readers would recognise the latter as a genuine prediction about the Roman Empire – explains why Daniel 8 is there at all. Look closely at Daniel 8 and you will see that almost everything it predicts is predicted in much more detail in Daniel 11 (see p. xvi). The only exception is its prediction of the cleansing of the Jewish temple (Daniel 8:14). Due to the fact that no specific details of this event are given, most scholars think this was a genuine prediction.

The temple was in fact cleansed around 164 BC, after the Jewish resistance fighters captured Jerusalem, so it could have been *ex eventu*. However, no hint of how that celebrated event came about appears in the book of Daniel; and there would have been such a desire amongst Jews at that time to restore the centre of their faith that it was a relatively safe bet that such an event would happen in the writer's near future. But whether it was genuine or not, that prediction could have been included within Daniel 11 *instead of* Daniel 8. It needn't have required a whole new prophecy. Hence, without the role of drawing the reader's attention to Daniel 7, and ensuring that this other animal prophecy gets interpreted as a prediction of the future (see p.60), a role it serves so remarkably well as we have seen, Daniel 8 would be rather redundant.

Whether or not it was these *ex eventu* prophecies that necessitated the inclusion of Daniel 2, 7 and 9, or the realisation that Daniel 2, 7 and 9 did not predict Antiochus Epiphanes that necessitated the writing of Daniel 8 and 11, or a bit of both, our conclusions about the origins of these prophecies remain. There is no valid reason to think that Daniel 2, 7 and 9 were anything but genuine predictions of the future. The absence of the name 'Rome' in Daniel 11 and 8 is easily explained as a consequence of diplomatic considerations. And the fact that the features of the eleventh horn in Daniel 7, and the 'Ruler who will come' in Daniel 9, bear some similarities to the portrayals of Antiochus Epiphanes in Daniel 8 and 11, can be very plausibly understood as a means of engaging the reader's interest in these genuine predictions. Were they really meant to predict Epiphanes, one would expect their writer to have done a far better job. It wouldn't have required much effort. All he'd need to do is remove two fallen horns from the fourth monster in Daniel 7 and make it come out of the third, and then swap a few words here and there: 'forty' in place of 'seventy', 'plunder' for 'destroy', 'the sanctuary' for 'an overspreading' in Daniel 9, and 'similar to' in place of 'different from' in Daniel 7. The fact that he has not can only mean he intended these prophecies to **predict the future**.

17. The Evidence of Josephus

By some incredible good fortune, the first-century Jewish historian Josephus twice escaped death to become an acquaintance and beneficiary of Vespasian (the eleventh king of the fourth empire from Daniel's time). In view of this, let's finish our discussion of the book of Daniel by considering what *he* wrote about Daniel 7.

The answer is *absolutely nothing!* Apart from a very brief allusion to it (see p.104) after his in-depth account of Daniel 1-6 and Daniel 8, he says not a word about it. Bearing in mind that Vespasian was his patron, this is not surprising. But it's only not surprising if **he believed Vespasian was the eleventh horn** (or thought that others would think this). That's because, from his detailed account of Daniel 2 *(Antiquities, X, 10:3-5)*, which he clearly regarded as predicting Rome, he thought highly of Daniel and was eager to show how his prophecies had been fulfilled. He would hardly have missed the opportunity Daniel 7 provided without good reason.

Josephus' comments on Daniel *(Antiquities, book X, ch.10-11)* are extremely pertinent because he was well acquainted with Jewish history. If anyone was capable of judging whether Antiochus Epiphanes could have been the eleventh horn in Daniel 7 or 'the

Ruler who will come' in Daniel 9 it was him. Moreover, it is rarely observed by critical scholars that, being on the payroll of the Roman emperors, Josephus had *an extremely strong motive* to interpret Daniel 2, 7 and 9 in the way that mainstream scholars do today. As we saw in chapters 9 and 10, Daniel 2 and Daniel 7 both predict the takeover of the Roman Empire by worshippers of *his God*. How embarrassing, and possibly even dangerous, that would be if word ever got out! As soon as his rival Roman intellectuals worked this out, he could be in serious trouble. **So it was definitely in his interests to suggest that these prophecies might have been about the Greek Empire and Antiochus Epiphanes**.

One would expect him, for example, to suggest that the second empire in Daniel 2 – the one represented by the statue's silver chest and arms – might actually constitute the empire of *Media alone* (just as mainstream scholars nowadays insist) rather than the Medo-Persian empire depicted by the two-horned ram in Daniel 8. And one would expect him to say something like "although everyone nowadays thinks the empire of bronze that will 'rule over all the earth' in Daniel 2 is the Greek Empire of Alexander, there is also a chance that this was meant to refer instead to the dominion of Persia (which was, after all, quite large too)".

To undermine the obvious counterarguments, he would no doubt have added…. "Yes, I know that empire is represented by a four-headed, four-winged leopard in Daniel 7, but these heads and wings needn't represent successor kingdoms. They could be… uhmmm… four Persian kings….or…uhm…the four corners of the earth to which the Persian Empire was maybe thought to extend…"

The fact that he does not even *hint* that this might have been the case, and instead merely chooses to remain silent about the embarrassing predictions in Daniel 7 and Daniel 9, is clear evidence that he felt this currently popular view was absolutely indefensible! Hopefully, this book has convinced you of this too.

18. If so, WHY?

If you have understood the significance of the observations in this book, and accept my assurances (ch.14) that the existence of a very real God – a universe-wide mind – is quite likely, you may now be somewhat more interested in Christianity than you were previously. One thing that might still be holding you back, though, is the question of motive. Why would that universe-wide mind *bother* giving us a message like that of Jesus?

According to that message, it is because God loves us and wants to *resurrect* us – to put us in charge of a new body at some point in the future (presumably furnished with our favourite memories of the life we're currently experiencing) – but only if we are willing to live forever in peace and harmony with him. But if God wanted to do that, couldn't 'he' do it *without* our consent? Why leave it up to us when the alternative is obviously not in our best interests?

You might be surprised to know that a possible answer to those questions emerges from the scientific explanation for our minds that I hinted at in chapter 14. To explain the complex organisation and biological information-carrying nature of our experiences as a product of Darwinian natural selection (as science suggests), there would have to exist other minds that *don't* carry such information – the ones from which ours evolved. And most of these minds will presumably never have had the opportunity to feel like an intelligent organism. They won't have been adapted to serve the function in a brain that we currently serve, and their experiences won't therefore have been shaped by the sort of neurological structures that currently shape ours. The reason God can't automatically resurrect us could simply be because he is committed to being fair. If we get a second such life, we are taking the place of a consciousness just like ourselves that has not yet had its *first* opportunity to feel like an intelligent organism.

Now you might think that this means God couldn't actually justify resurrecting *any* of us. There is, however, a way around this problem that doesn't negate the righteousness that is central to the Christian concept of God. As well as choosing to be fair to other consciousnesses, God might also have chosen to abide by certain rules that take precedence over fairness. He might, for example, have chosen to 'only do to other consciousnesses what he would have them do to him if he were in their situation'; and to 'minimise suffering', *in that order* (they'd have to be in that order in view of the amount of suffering evident in the world). If those priorities take precedence over fairness, we can understand why a righteous God might be able to justify resurrecting consciousnesses who are committed to living forever in peace and harmony. Provided those consciousnesses fear what is to happen to them after death, God could justify the *promise* of resurrection as a way of alleviating this form of suffering (without harming the sufferer). And, in view of his primary commitment to 'do unto others…', he won't give false hope. He wouldn't want to be given false hope if he were in our shoes. He can thus fulfil that promise without compromising his righteousness through any unjustified lack of fairness.

To explain the gospel message, only one further assumption is needed: God must be ensuring that consciousnesses at all times have free will. That explains why he gives us a choice. His commitment to minimising suffering is why he wants to resurrect only people who are likewise committed to doing good for other consciousnesses – though, as the gospels make clear, our *human ability* in that department is irrelevant. It is our *willingness* (shown through repentance and kind, self-sacrificing acts) that matters.

Whatever you make of these ideas, it's worth remembering that if God is real, and can 'see your thoughts', as our observations in this book appear to require, you should be able to speak to him directly. He is obviously the best person to answer your questions. Judging from my own experience, if you pray earnestly and seriously, and persist in doing so, it will not be long before these answers come to you. Hopefully, my observations in this book have given you some reason to do this.

Remember, Daniel 7 (with Daniel 2) accurately predicted that the eleventh king of the fourth distinct empire in the sequence beginning with Babylon – an empire that would crush a four-part-divided empire that previously ruled the world! – would *subdue three previous kings of his kingdom, make war upon worshippers of the Jewish God,* and *speak words against the Most High (a Jewish religious leader whose followers would later take over that fourth empire).* Whatever critical scholars say about the origin of this passage, this very precise prediction was **undeniably fulfilled by Vespasian's rise to power in *The Year of the Four Emperors,* his conquest of the Jews, and his use of a Jewish Messianic prophecy as propaganda justifying his claim to power** (ch.11).

Remember also that Daniel 9 specifies a very long time period that was **definitely meant to start with Nehemiah's Permission to rebuild Jerusalem in 444 BC** (see ch.4), **and end with a Christ who'd be an exalted leader, and get put to death.** And one of only three plausible meanings of that time period (ch.6) ends within at most a month of Christ's Triumphal Entry in 33 AD!

That is incredibly unlikely to be chance! But this shocking accuracy doesn't end there. The latter prophecy also predicted a simultaneous destruction of Jerusalem and her Temple after the end of that time period (ch.7) – fulfilled perfectly in 70 AD. And to the absolute astonishment of anyone familiar with Jewish history, it also predicted that a ruler of the same people responsible for that destruction of Jerusalem would, for the last seven years of his life, fulfil a 'promise' he had made 'to many' (which in the context of this prophecy can only mean *a commitment to rebuild Jerusalem*), in the middle of which he would end Jewish sacrifice and offering and raise a foreign idol on an infamous overspreading. All this was perfectly fulfilled by the Roman Emperor Hadrian (see ch.7).

Don't be misled by the frequent suggestion of critical scholars that this was just history repeating itself – that predictions of Antiochus Epiphanes are here being reinterpreted. There is no question about the fact that these passages *never ever* predicted Epiphanes. Nor is there any reason to think they were ever intended to. But if they were, their writer made massive mistakes in his account of history, and these unlikely errors just happened to make his account accurately predict very specific future events pertaining to the rise of Christianity. Did God do that? Perhaps it is time you asked Him.

> Whatever you may ask of the Father in my name,
> he will give it to you.
> Until now, you have asked nothing in my name.
> Ask, and you will receive, that your joy may be made complete.
> I have spoken these things to you in figures of speech.
> But the time is coming when I will no more speak to you
> in figures of speech, but will tell you plainly about the Father.
> In that day you will ask in my name;
> and I don't say to you that I will pray to the Father for you,
> for the Father himself loves you, because you have loved me,
> and have believed that I came from God.

John 16:23-27

Additional Observations

The Flood in Daniel 9:26 (ch.7): A flood was a common metaphor for a full-scale war (see Daniel 11:40). If the subject of 'His end will come with a flood' is *the Ruler who will come* (which is less popular with interpreters, but clearly far more consistent with 'the end that is determined' being poured out on that ruler in verse 27), then it can be unambiguously identified as *Hadrian's war against the Jews*. His end did come with that flood because he died only a couple of years afterwards – and though the fighting was finished, his oppression of the Jews was still ongoing.

The Continuation of War in Daniel 9:26 (ch.7): Interpreting the flood in Daniel 9:26 as 'war' is supported by the reference to ongoing war in the next sentence. However, since that flood refers specifically to the war that characterises the final few years of *the Ruler who will come*, the 'continuation' in that other reference to war should probably be interpreted as 'including the time from the destruction of Jerusalem until that final war'. If so, it can be very satisfyingly identified as the oppression and unrest that characterised the relationship between Jews and Romans from 70 AD until 132 AD, which peaked in the widespread uprisings of 115-117, known as the *Kitos* War.

The Bear for Persia in Daniel 7:5 (ch.8): The name *Dobiel* meaning *'bear god'* for the guardian angel of Persia in the Talmud (*Yoma* 77a) is justifiably believed to be based upon Daniel 7. But what inspired the author of Daniel 7 to represent Persia by a bear? Size, strength or ferocity are not attributes that were unique to Persia; and clearly, it seems the early Jewish interpreters attached *religious* significance to the animal types. Nevertheless, there appear to be no bears in the Zoroastrian religion of the Persians. My guess is that the writer of Daniel 7 thought the name 'Persia' – originally pronounced 'Paarsa' – meant 'Protected by bears'. 'Pa' definitely meant 'protected' in Old Persian (Kent, p.194), and 'arsa' could have meant 'bear' (Bartholomae 1904, p.204).

The Bronze claws (Daniel 7:19, ch.11) that *trampled the residue* are a startlingly appropriate symbol for Rome's hated *tax farmers* (the 'tax collectors' of the New Testament).

The 'times' (Daniel 7:25, ch.12): The Jubilee cycle (Leviticus 25:10, p.46) was interpreted by the Jews as a 49-year cycle with the fiftieth year being the first year of the next cycle. This meant there'd never be two adjacent *years of rest* for the land. However, 'fifty years' is still the literal meaning of the scripture (see * p.88). As in Daniel 9, a literal meaning has probably been chosen to render claims of self-fulfilment implausible.

The Silver arms, and Bronze belly & thighs (Daniel 2:32, ch.10) could stand for the Persians and Medes (the silver arms), and Macedon with the Seleucid and Ptolemaic empires (the bronze belly and thighs). Whether the relatively small Greek kingdom of Pergamon was also represented on the statue is anybody's guess!

The Two Iron legs (Daniel 2:33, ch.10): As a symbol of the Roman Republic – by far the dominant nation in 165 BC – the number of these could signify the fact that the head of the Roman Republic was usually a *pair* of annually elected *consuls*.

The Iron legs and Iron & Clay Feet (Daniel 2:33, ch.10): Although it could not have been apparent to readers in 165 BC, the Roman empire was destined to have *two distinct phases of government* (The Republic and The Emperors); and the latter phase would be typified by an influx of non-Romans into the army (and, through marriage, political office). Being loyal firstly to their local commander, this allowed frequent civil war, and hence weakness.

The Stone (Daniel 2:34-35, ch.10): The stone cut out of a mountain 'without hands', which strikes the statue on its iron and clay feet before becoming 'a mountain filling the whole earth', is *a highly appropriate symbol for Jesus Christ* – the founder of Christianity who called himself 'the stone the builders have rejected' (Matthew 21:42, Acts 4:11).

The Four-Kingdoms Vision in Daniel 2 (Daniel 2:31-45, ch.10): Since almost all the historical content of this vision could have been taken from Daniel 7 (including its prediction of the eternal, worldwide kingdom of God), it is reasonable to speculate on whether it might have been written later than Daniel 7 and derived from that passage. There are, however, certain arguments against this possibility: Firstly, Daniel 7 has crucial features that are notably absent from Daniel 2: The part of the statue representing the third kingdom in Daniel 2 doesn't show an obvious four-way division like the third beast in Daniel 7. Nor is there any attempt in Daniel 2 to portray the eleventh king of the fourth empire. Secondly, Daniel 2 does contain historical information that *isn't* found in Daniel 7 – especially concerning the first three empires: Through Daniel's deliberately flattering description of the statue's gold head as "You, O king", we learn that the first kingdom is Babylon. Daniel 2 also says that the third kingdom would 'rule over all the earth' – a statement that would clearly have identified it as *Greece* in the minds of Jews living in the Greek world of 165 BC. Moreover, it is only in Daniel 2 that the fourth kingdom is predicted to have two phases, and the emergent religion of the holy people (the world-filling mountain) is predicted to be fashioned out of Moses-based Judaism (the mountain from which the stone was cut). Hence, it seems clear to me that Daniel 7 was written later than Daniel 2 and is designed to complement it with further detail.

But why wouldn't the writer responsible for Daniel 7 not put all the necessary details in that passage as well, thereby eliminating the need to preserve both prophecies? One possible reason is that perhaps Daniel 2 is making the one prediction that God really *wants* to fulfil as its only specific prediction of the future. It predicts the formation of a new worldwide religion out of Judaism during the second phase of the Roman Empire. Perhaps that is the primary prediction God wants to make – the others being merely secondary predictions designed to show (through fulfilment) that this primary prediction can only have come from God. Due to the fact that the fulfilment of this prediction might not seem anything very surprising, a second prophecy (Daniel 7) was constructed that made a really specific prediction that could not be self-fulfilled – the replacement of three earlier kings by the eleventh of the fourth empire. The fulfilment of this prediction would be an indisputable sign that this prophecy was from God. And just to make absolutely sure, the really specific predictions of Daniel 9 were then added, and claims of hindsight rendered unreasonable by the inclusion of Daniel 8 and Daniel 11. Nevertheless, Daniel 2 was kept because it shows what the primary prediction is: The rise of Christianity.

The Role of Daniel 8 and 11 (ch.2): Some Christian interpreters have invoked a 'day-for-a-year' principle to claim that the time periods in Daniel 8 and Daniel 10-12 (2300, 1290, 1335 days) make these prophecies predict the future even today. The main problem I have with this claim is that Daniel 11 contains errors; and if forgeries, both these passages also contain *lies*. Any fulfilment of them would make God appear to err and lie. Hence I think they are purely there to ensure that Daniel 2, 7 and 9 *cannot be reasonably argued to be hindsight* – a role they fulfil perfectly.

APPENDIX

Extracts from Daniel 8, Daniel 10-12 and Nehemiah 9

1. *Ex eventu* Prophecies of Antiochus Epiphanes

Daniel 8: Set on the banks of a river called Ulai in the citadel of Susa, Daniel 8:3-14 (the ram and goat vision) says the following:

> **Dan 8:3-14** [3]...Behold, there stood before the river a ram which had two horns. The two horns were high; but **one was higher than the other**, and the higher came up last. [4]I saw the ram pushing westward, northward, and southward. No animals could stand before him. There wasn't any who could deliver out of his hand; but he did according to his will, and magnified himself. [5]As I was considering, behold, a male goat came from the west over the surface of the whole earth, and didn't touch the ground. The goat had a notable horn between his eyes [6]He came to the ram that had the two horns, which I saw standing before the river, and ran on him in the fury of his power. [7]I saw him come close to the ram, and he was moved with anger against him, and struck the ram, and broke his two horns. There was no power in the ram to stand before him; but he cast him down to the ground, and trampled on him. There was no one who could deliver the ram out of his hand. [8]The male goat magnified himself exceedingly. When he was strong, the great horn was broken; and in its place grew **four notable horns toward the four winds of heaven**.

⁹**Out of one of them emerged a little horn**, which grew exceedingly great, toward the south, and toward the east, and toward the glorious land. ¹⁰It grew great, even to the army of heaven; and it cast down some of the army and of the stars to the ground, and trampled on them. ¹¹Yes, it magnified itself, even to the prince of the army; and it **took away from him the continual burnt offering, and the place of his sanctuary was cast down**. ¹²The army was given over to it together with the continual burnt offering through disobedience. It cast down truth to the ground, and did its pleasure and prospered. ¹³Then I heard a holy one speaking; and another said to the one who spoke, "How long will it last: the vision about the continual burnt offering, and the disobedience that makes desolate, and the giving of both the sanctuary and the army to be trodden under foot?" ¹⁴He said to me, "To two thousand three hundred evenings and mornings. Then the sanctuary will be cleansed."

Daniel 8:20-25 interprets the imagery in this vision as follows:

<u>**Dan 8:20-25**</u> ²⁰The ram which you saw, that had the two horns, is the kings [kingdoms] of Media and Persia. ²¹The rough male goat is the king [kingdom] of Greece. **The great horn that is between his eyes is the first king** [Alexander the Great]. ²²As for that which was broken, in the place of which four rose up, **four kingdoms will rise up out of his nation, but not with his power.** ²³In the latter time of their kingdom, when the transgressors have come to the full, **a king of fierce face, and understanding dark sentences** [Antiochus Epiphanes], will arise. ²⁴His power will be mighty, **but not by his own power**. He will destroy awesomely, and will prosper in what he does. He will destroy the mighty ones and the holy people. ²⁵Through his policy he will cause deceit to prosper in his hand. He will magnify himself in his heart, and he will destroy many in their security. **He will also rise up against the prince of princes**; but he will be broken without hand.

Daniel 11: The prophecy of the sanctuary's defilement in Daniel 8:11 is repeated in Daniel 11:31, below. After an *ex eventu* prediction of Antiochus Epiphanes' rise to power (with no mention of any deposed kings – see p.128) and his successful first war against Egypt, Daniel 11:29-35 says the following:

> **Dan 11:29-35** [29]He [Epiphanes] will return at the appointed time, and come into the south [Egypt]; but it won't be in the latter time as it was in the former. [30]For **ships of Kittim [Rome] will come against him**. Therefore he will be grieved, and will return, and have indignation against the holy covenant [the Jewish religion], and will take action. He will even return, and have regard to those who forsake the holy covenant. **[31]Forces will rise on his part, and they will profane the sanctuary [the Jerusalem Temple], even the fortress, and will take away the continual burnt offering. Then they will set up the abomination that makes desolate.** [32]He will corrupt those who do wickedly against the covenant by flatteries; but the people who know their God will be strong and take action. [33]Those who are wise among the people will instruct many; yet they will fall by the sword and by flame, by captivity and by plunder, for many days [the persecution at the time of writing]. [34]Now when they fall, they will receive a little help; but many will join themselves to them with flatteries. [35]Some of those who are wise will fall, to refine them, and to purify, and to make them white, even to the time of the end…

Daniel 11 finishes with a *real prediction* (v.40-45), which failed to come true because Epiphanes did not invade Egypt a third time:

> **Dan 11:40-45** [40]At the time of the end the king of the south will contend with him [the king of the north]; and the king of the north will come against him [the king of the south] like a whirlwind, with chariots, with horsemen, and with many ships. He will enter into the countries, and will overflow and pass

through [i.e. like a flood]. ⁴¹He will enter also into the glorious land [Israel], and many countries will be overthrown; but these will be delivered out of his hand: Edom, Moab, and the chief of the children of Ammon. ⁴²He will also stretch out his hand on the countries. **The land of Egypt won't escape**. ⁴³He will have power over the treasures of gold and of silver, and over all the precious things of Egypt. The Libyans and the Ethiopians will be at his steps.⁴⁴But news out of the east and out of the north will trouble him; and he will go out with great fury to destroy and utterly to sweep away many. ⁴⁵He will plant the tents of his palace between the sea and the glorious holy mountain; yet he will come to his end, and no one will help him.

Daniel 12: The *king of the north* in the above prediction must still be Epiphanes because, after predicting a time of trouble to follow this king's death, and having an angel ask about its length, Daniel 12 gives the time from Epiphanes' Temple desecration as follows:

Dan 12:11 ¹¹From the time that the continual burnt offering is taken away, and the abomination that makes desolate set up [as predicted in Daniel 11:31 – see p.123], there will be **one thousand two hundred ninety** *days*. [i.e. just over 3.5 years]

We know this is the time for *all* those events (and an interpretation of the phrase 'a time, times and half a time') because this verse is given as an explanation of Daniel 12:6-7, which says:

Dan 12:6-7 ⁶[An angel] said to the man clothed in linen, who was above the waters of the river [a fiery-eyed angel], **"How long will it be to the end of these wonders?"** ⁷The man clothed in linen, who was above the waters of the river, held up his right hand and his left hand to heaven, and I heard him swear by him who lives forever that it will be **for a time, times, and a half**; when they have finished breaking in pieces the power of the holy people, all these things will be finished.

2. References to Rome in Daniel 11

There are two allusions to the dominance of Rome in Daniel 11. One is Daniel 11:30, shown earlier on page 123. Although the location 'Kittim' in that verse refers generally to the Mediterranean islands and coastlands west of what is now Turkey, the ships can only be those carrying the Roman ambassador Popilius Laenas, as it was his confrontation with Epiphanes near Alexandria in 168 BC that caused the latter's withdrawal from Egypt. The story goes that Epiphanes asked for time to consider what to do. But Popilius drew a line round him in the sand and ordered him to give his decision to the Senate before crossing that line. With the Romans having recently subdued the rebellious kingdom of Macedon, Epiphanes wisely chose to withdraw. Since subject peoples were bound to interpret this as a sign of weakness, he was in a situation where he probably felt he had to make an example of someone, and the Jews happened to be in the wrong place at the wrong time.

The other reference that has to be to Rome is Daniel 11:18, which comes at the end of a passage "predicting" the military campaigns of Antiochus III (Epiphanes' father). It says the following:

> [18]After this he will turn his face to the islands, and will take many; but a commander will cause the reproach offered by him to cease. Yes, moreover, he will turn his reproach back on him.

This verse can only be referring to Antiochus III's defeat by Rome. The first sentence may be referring to the Battle of Thermopylae in 191 BC, which put an end to his invasion of Greece, and the second to his decisive defeat on his own territory at Magnesia. Although two different Roman commanders were responsible, the writer may have thought there was only one. Alternatively, it could refer to the Battle of Magnesia and the Peace of Apamea, the treaty that made the Seleucid Empire subject to Rome. Both events clearly betray the supremacy of Rome in the writer's world.

3. Extracts from Nehemiah 9 relating to Daniel 9:16

The two extracts below show the parts of the second prayer in the book of Nehemiah that the writer of Daniel 9 may have been alluding to with his use of the words 'righteous acts' and 'object of scorn' in Daniel 9:16 (see p.29).

God's 'Righteous Acts' in Nehemiah 9:27-31 [27]…In the time of their trouble, when they cried to you, you heard from heaven; and according to your manifold mercies you gave them saviours who saved them out of the hands of their adversaries. [28]But after they had rest, they did evil again before you; therefore you left them in the hands of their enemies, so that they had the dominion over them; yet when they returned, and cried to you, you heard from heaven; and many times you delivered them according to your mercies, [29]and testified against them, that you might bring them again to your law. Yet they were arrogant, and didn't listen to your commandments, but sinned against your ordinances (which if a man does, he shall live in them), turned their backs, stiffened their neck, and would not hear. [30]Yet many years you put up with them, and testified against them by your Spirit through your prophets. Yet they would not give ear. Therefore you gave them into the hand of the peoples of the lands. [31]Nevertheless in your manifold mercies you didn't make a full end of them, nor forsake them; for you are a gracious and merciful God.

Israel as an 'Object of Scorn' in Nehemiah 9:36-37 [36]Behold, we are servants today, and as for the land that you gave to our fathers to eat its fruit and its good, behold, we are servants in it. [37]It yields much increase to the kings whom you have set over us because of our sins. Also they have power over our bodies and over our livestock, at their pleasure, and we are in great distress.

4. Details of the Syrian Wars in Daniel 11:5-21

The extract below shows the detailed history in Daniel 11 (p.xvi).

[For v.2-4, see p.10] [5]The king of the south [Ptolemy I] will be strong. One of his princes [Seleucus I] will become stronger than him, and have dominion. His dominion will be a great dominion. [6]At the end of years they will join themselves together; and the daughter [Berenice] of the king of the south [Ptolemy II] will come to the king of the north [Antiochus II] to make an agreement; but she will not retain the strength of her arm. He will also not stand, nor will his arm; but she will be given up, with those who brought her, and he who became the father of her, and he who strengthened her in those times.[7]But out of a shoot from her roots one will stand up in his place [her brother Ptolemy III], who will come to the army, and will enter into the fortress of the king of the north [Seleucus II], and deal against them, and prevail. [8]He will also carry their gods, with their molten images, and with their goodly vessels of silver and of gold, captive into Egypt. He will refrain some years from the king of the north. [9]He [Seleucus II] will come into the realm of the king of the south, but he will return into his own land. [10]His sons will wage war, and will assemble a multitude of great forces, which will come on, and overflow, and pass through. They will return and wage war, even to his fortress.

[11]The king of the south [Ptolemy IV] will be moved with anger, and will come out and fight with him, even with the king of the north. He [Antiochus III] will send out a great multitude, and the multitude will be given into his [Ptolemy IV's] hand [Battle of Raphia 217 BC]. [12]The multitude will be lifted up, and his heart will be exalted. He will cast down tens of thousands, but he won't prevail. [13]The king of the north [Antiochus III, again] will return, and will send out a multitude greater than the former. He will invade at the end of the times, even of years [around 200 BC], with a great army and with much substance.

[14]In those times many will stand up against the king of the south [Ptolemy V]. Also the children of the violent among your people will lift themselves up to establish the vision [what vision? – this one presumably wasn't around then]; but they will fall. [15]So the king of the north [Antiochus III] will come and cast up a mound, and take a well-fortified city. The forces of the [king of the] south won't stand [Battle of Panium – 200 BC], neither will his chosen people, neither will there be any strength left to stand. [16]But he who comes against him will do as he pleases, and no one will stand before him. He will stand in the glorious land, and destruction will be in his hand [From 200 BC Judea came under Seleucid rather than Ptolemaic rule].

[17]He [Antiochus III] will set his face to come with the strength of his whole kingdom, and bring equitable conditions. He [Ptolemy V] will perform them. He [Antiochus III] will give him the daughter of women [his daughter Cleopatra I], to corrupt her [make her act deceitfully for his purposes]; but she will not stand, and won't be for him. [18]After this he will turn his face to the islands, and will take many; but a prince [Roman general] will cause the reproach offered by him to cease. Yes, moreover, he will cause his reproach to turn on him [Battle of Magnesia]. [19]Then he will turn his face toward the fortresses of his own land; but he will stumble and fall, and won't be found.

[20]Then one who will cause a tax collector to pass through the kingdom to maintain its glory will stand up in his place [Seleucus IV]; but within few days he shall be destroyed, not in anger, and not in battle. [21]In his place a contemptible person [Antiochus IV Epiphanes] will stand up, to whom they had not given the honour of the kingdom; but he will come in time of security, and will obtain the kingdom by flatteries.

Those who insist on claiming that this part of the book of Daniel is divine prophecy should ask themselves: Would a loving God really call anyone a 'contemptible person' – even Antiochus Epiphanes?

SELECTIVE BIBLIOGRAPHY

Ager, S. L. (2003), An Uneasy Balance: From the Death of Seleukos to the Battle of Raphia, in Erskine, A. ed. (2005), *A Companion to the Hellenistic World* (UK: Blackwell), 35-50.

Albertz, R. (2002), The Social Setting of the Aramaic and Hebrew Book of Daniel, in Collins, J. J. & Flint, P. W. eds. (2002), *The Book of Daniel: Composition and Reception,* Vol. I (Brill Academic Publishers), 171-204.

Anderson, Robert (1894/1918), *The Coming Prince* (Philologos Edition 2002) http://philologos.org/__eb-tcp/preface.htm.

Armstrong, K. (1993/1999), *A History of God* (London: Vintage).

Arrian of Nicomedia (early 2nd century AD), *Anabasis: The Campaigns of Alexander*, trans. by Aubrey de Sélincourt (1958) (UK: Penguin classics).

Austin, M. (2003), The Seleukids and Asia, in Erskine, A. ed. (2005) *A Companion to the Hellenistic World* (UK: Blackwell), 121-133.

Barr, J. (1962), Daniel, in *Peake's Commentary on the Bible*, Rowley H. H. & Black, M., eds. (Great Britain: Thomas Nelson & Sons), 591-602.

Bartholomae, C. (1904). *Altiranisches worterbuch* (Strassburg: Verlag von Karl J. Trubner)

Barton, J. (2002), Theological Ethics in Daniel, in Collins, J. J. & Flint, P. W. eds. (2002), *The Book of Daniel, Composition and Reception,* Vol. II (Brill Academic Publishers), 661-670.

Boccaccini, G. (2002), The Solar Calendars of Daniel and Enoch, in Collins, J. J. & Flint, P. W. eds. (2002), *The Book of Daniel, Composition and Reception,* Vol. II (Brill Academic Publishers), 311-328.

Braund, D. (2003), After Alexander: the Emergence of the Hellenistic World, in Erskine, A. ed. (2005), *A Companion to the Hellenistic World* (UK: Blackwell),19-34.

Browne, L. E. (1962), Ezra & Nehemiah, in *Peake's Commentary on the Bible*, Rowley H. H. & Black, M., eds. (Great Britain: Thomas Nelson & Sons), 370-380.

Chaniotis, A. (2003), The Divinity of Hellenistic Rulers, in Erskine, A. ed. (2005), *A Companion to the Hellenistic World* (UK: Blackwell), 431-445.

Collins, J. J. (1984), *Daniel with an Introduction to Apocalyptic Literature* (Michigan, USA: Eerdmans Publishing Company).

Collins, J. J. & Flint, P. W. eds. (2002), *The Book of Daniel: Composition & Reception,* Vols I & II (Brill Academic Publishers).

Collins, J. J. (2002), Current Issues in the Study of Daniel, in Collins, J. J. & Flint, P. W. eds. (2002), *The Book of Daniel, Composition and Reception,* Vol. I (Brill Academic Publishers), 3-15.

Clark K. W. (1960), Worship in the Jerusalem Temple after A.D. 70, *New Testament Studies* 6(4), 1960, 269-280.

Curtis, J. ed. (1997/2005), *Mesopotamia and Iran in the Persian Period*, (Great Britain: British Museum Press).

Danziger, D. & Purcell, N. (2005), *Hadrian's Empire: When Rome Ruled the World* (Great Britain: Hodder & Stoughton).

Derow, P. (2003), The Arrival of Rome: From the Illyrian Wars to the Fall of Macedon, in Erskine, A. ed. (2005), *A Companion to the Hellenistic World* (UK: Blackwell), 51-70.

Di Lella A. A. (2002), The Textual History of Septuagint-Daniel and Theodotion-Daniel, in Collins, J. J. & Flint, P. W. eds. (2002), *The Book of Daniel, Composition and Reception,* Vol. II (Brill Academic Publishers), 586-607.

Dio, Cassius (c 230) *Roman History, books 63-69* (Online edition 2004 translated by Herbert B. Foster, http://www.gutenberg.org/files/10890/ 10890-h/10890-h.htm).

Diodorus Siculus (c 59 BC), *Bibliotheca Historica,* Loeb Classical Library translation (1954) Online edition at LacusCurtius http://penelope.uchicago. edu/Thayer/E/Roman/Texts/Diodorus_Siculus/home.html

Eddington. A. S. (1928), *The Nature of the Physical World* (New York: The Macmillan Company).

Eilers, C. (2003), A Roman East: Pompey's Settlement to the Death of Augustus, in Erskine, A. ed. (2005), *A Companion to the Hellenistic World* (UK: Blackwell), 90-102.

Erskine, A. ed. (2005), *A Companion to the Hellenistic World* (UK: Blackwell).

Eshel, E. (2002), Possible Sources of the Book of Daniel, in Collins, J. J. & Flint, P. W. eds. (2002), *The Book of Daniel, Composition and Reception,* Vol. II (Brill Academic Publishers), 387-394.

Eusebius Pamphili (c 325-39), *Church History, Life of Constantine, and Oration in Praise of Constantine* (E-book published by B&R Samizdat Express).

Eusebius Pamphili (c.325/2008), *Chronicon,* Book I, translated by Andrew Smith www.tertullian.org/fathers/eusebius_chronicon_01_text.htm

Evans, C.A (2002), Daniel in the New Testament, in Collins, J. J. & Flint, P. W. eds. (2002), *The Book of Daniel, Composition and Reception,* Vol. II (Brill Academic Publishers), 491-527.

Faulkner, N. (2004), *Apocalypse: The Great Jewish Revolt Against Rome AD66-73* (Gloucestershire, UK: Tempus Publishing Ltd).

Flint, P. W. (2002), The Daniel Tradition at Qumran, in Collins, J. J. & Flint, P. W. eds. (2002), *The Book of Daniel, Composition and Reception,* Vol. II (Brill Academic Publishers), 329-367.

Ghalekhani, G. & Khaksar, M. (2016), A Thematic and Etymological Glossary of Carnivorous Animals Based on the Pahlavi Text of Iranian Bundahishn, *Biological Forum* 8(1): 287-294.

Grabbe, L. L. (2002), A Dan(iel) For All Seasons: For Whom was Daniel Important?, in Collins, J. J. & Flint, P. W. eds. (2002), *The Book of Daniel, Composition and Reception,* Vol. I (Brill Academic Publishers), 229-246.

Gruen, E. S. (2003), Jews and Greeks, in Erskine, A. ed. (2005), *A Companion to the Hellenistic World* (UK: Blackwell), 263-279.

Herodotus (c 450-420 BC), *The Histories,* Penguin Classics 2003 edition (London: Penguin Books Ltd).

Hoehner, H. (1973/1977), *Chronological Aspects of the Life of Christ* (USA: Zondervan).

Holland, T. (2005), *Persian Fire: The First World Empire and the Battle for the West* (Great Britain: Abacus).

Holland, T. (2007), *Rubicon: The Triumph and Tragedy of the Roman Republic* (Great Britain: Abacus)

Jerome (c 407), *Commentary on Daniel,* trans. by Gleason. L. Archer, Jr (1958) (Michigan, USA: Baker Book House), http://www.tertullian.org/fathers/jerome_daniel_01_intro.htm.

Josephus, Flavius (c 94/1737), *Antiquities of the Jews,* trans. by William Whiston, (E-book Electronically Developed by MobileReference).

Josephus, Flavius (c 75/1981), *The Jewish War* (London: Penguin Books Ltd).

Kent, R. G. (1950), *Old Persian: Grammar, Texts, Lexicon* (USA: American Oriental Society), 194.

Kitchen, K. A. (1965), The Aramaic of Daniel, in Wiseman, D. J., ed., *Notes on Some Problems in the Book of Daniel* (London: The Tyndale Press), 31-79.

Knib, M. A. (2002), The Book of Daniel in its Context, in Collins, J. J. & Flint, P. W. eds. (2002), *The Book of Daniel, Composition and Reception,* Vol. I (Brill Academic Publishers), 16-35.

Knight, G. A. F. (1971), The Book of Daniel, in *The Interpreter's One Volume Commentary on the Bible* (Great Britain: Abingdon Press), 436-450.

Koch, K. (2002), Stages in the Canonization of the Book of Daniel, in Collins, J. J. & Flint, P. W. eds. (2002), *The Book of Daniel, Composition and Reception,* Vol. II (Brill Academic Publishers), 421-446.

Kosmetatou, E. (2003), The Attalids of Pergamon, in Erskine, A. ed. (2005) *A Companion to the Hellenistic World* (UK: Blackwell), 159-174.

Kratz, R. G. (2002), The Visions of Daniel, in Collins, J. J. & Flint, P. W. eds. (2002), *The Book of Daniel, Composition and Reception,* Vol. I (Brill Academic Publishers), 91-113.

Kriwaczek, P. (2012), *Babylon: Mesopotamia and the Birth of Civilisation* (Great Britain: Atlantic Books).

Livius, Titus (27-09BC/1905), *The History of Rome, Vols 1-6,* Books 1-10 & 21-45, Rhys, E. ed. trans. by Rev. C. Roberts (London: J. M. Dent & Sons).

Lust, J. (2002), Cult and Sacrifice in Daniel: The Tamid and the Abomination of Desolation, in Collins, J. J. & Flint, P. W. eds. (2002), *The Book of Daniel, Composition and Reception,* Vol. II (Brill Academic Publishers), 671-688.

Ma, J. (2003), Kings, in Erskine, A. ed. (2005), *A Companion to the Hellenistic World* (UK: Blackwell), 179-195.

McGing, B. (2003), Subjection and Resistance: to the Death of Mithradates, in Erskine, A. ed. (2005), *A Companion to the Hellenistic World* (UK: Blackwell), 71-89.

Mitchel, T. C., (1997), Achaemenid History and the Book of Daniel, in Curtis, J. ed. (1997/2005), *Mesopotamia and Iran in the Persian Period,* London: British Museum Press, 68-78.

Montefiore, S. S. (2011), *Jerusalem: The Biography* (Great Britain: Phoenix).

Morwood, J. (2013), *Hadrian* (Great Britain: Bloomsbury Academic).

Newton, Isaac (1733), *Observations upon the Prophecies of Daniel and the Apocalypse of St John* (London: Darby & Browne, Repr. 2005 as e-book at http://www.gutenberg.org).

Paul, S. M. (2002), The Mesopotamian Background of Daniel 1-6, in Collins, J. J. & Flint, P. W. eds. (2002), *The Book of Daniel, Composition and Reception,* Vol. I (Brill Academic Publishers), 55-68.

Peterson, J. H. ed. (1995), Avesta:Yashts (Hymns of praise): XIV Wharharan Yasht, online edition http://www.avesta.org/ka/yt14sbe.htm, trans. by James Darmesteter (*Sacred Books of the East*, American Edition, 1898).

Polybius (c 160 BC), *The Histories, Book XXI* (Loeb Classical Library Edition vol 5, 1922 thru 1927, 237-343).

Porteous, N. (1965), *Daniel: Old Testament Library* (London: SCM Press Ltd).

Potter, D. (2003), Hellenistic Religion, in Erskine, A. ed. (2005), *A Companion to the Hellenistic World* (UK: Blackwell), 407-430.

Potter, D. (2011), *Emperors of Rome* (London: Quercus Publishing plc)

Rogerson, J. (2001), *The Oxford Illustrated History of the Bible* (Great Britain: Oxford University Press).

Rogerson, J. & Davies, P. R. (2005), *The Old Testament World* (London: T & T Clark International).

Schama, S. (2014), *The Story of the Jews* (London: Vintage).

Scullard, H. H. (1970), *From the Gracchi to Nero: A History of Rome from 133 BC to AD 68* (London: University Paperback, Methuen & Co Ltd).

Seutonius (c 120) *The Lives of the Twelve Caesars* (Online edition produced by Tapio Riikonen and David Widger http://www.gutenberg.org/files/6400/6400-h/6400-h.htm).

Shea, W. H. (1982) Darius the Mede: An Update, *Andrews University Seminary Studies,* Autumn 1982, *Vol.* 20, No. 3, 229-247 (http://www.auss.info/auss_publication_file.php?pub_id=654).

Stephenson, P. (2009/2011), *Constantine* (London: Quercus).

Tacitus (c 109) *The Histories* (Online edition: Translated by Alfred John Church and William J. Brodribb http://classics.mit.edu/Tacitus/histories.html).

Thompson, D. J. (2003), The Ptolemies and Egypt, in Erskine, A. ed. (2005), *A Companion to the Hellenistic World* (UK: Blackwell), 105-120.

Ulrich, E. (2002), The Text of Daniel in the Qumran Scrolls, in Collins, J. J. & Flint, P. W. eds. (2002), *The Book of Daniel, Composition and Reception,* Vol. II (Brill Academic Publishers), 573-585.

Vermes, Geza (2004), *The Complete Dead Sea Scrolls in English*, (London: Penguin Classics, Penguin Books Ltd).

Wesselius, Jan-Wim (2002), The Writing of Daniel, in Collins, J. J. & Flint, P. W. eds. (2002), *The Book of Daniel, Composition and Reception,* Vol. II (Brill Academic Publishers), 291-310.

Wilson, M. R. (1989/1995), *Our Father Abraham: Jewish Roots of the Christian Faith* (Eerdmans Publishing Company, Grand Rapids, Michigan and Centre for Judaic Christian Studies, Dayton, Ohio).

Xenophon (c 360 BC), *Cyropaedia* (Project Gutenberg E-book, trans. H.G. Dakyns, ed. F.M. Stawell).

INDEX

ACKNOWLEDGEMENTS

This book has been a long time in preparation, and its Bibliography comes nowhere near to reflecting the quantity of research that has gone into it. I must therefore thank all the unmentioned creators of websites on Daniel and related topics that I have perused over the years. I owe a considerable debt of gratitude to Rev. Bill McDonald for the loan of several books, and to Marco Agolini for his helpful feedback on my first attempt at writing this one. I am also deeply indebted to Ruth for reading all my earlier versions of this book and offering constant encouragement and support, and to Jim for our lengthy discussions covering many of the ideas that this book now contains. I also owe a debt of gratitude to Alison for her helpful feedback, and to Fiona and Amie for helping me finally get this work into print. Most of all, though, my deepest gratitude is owed as always to the God of Daniel without whose astonishing inspiration I would not have had a book to write.

The Epicureans are in error, who cast Providence out of human life,
and do not believe that God takes care of the affairs of the world,
nor that the universe is governed and continued in being
by that blessed and immortal nature,
but say that the world is carried along of its own accord,
without a ruler and a curator…
were it destitute of a guide to conduct it, as they imagine,
it would be like ships without pilots, which we see drowned by the winds,
or like chariots without drivers, which are overturned;
so would the world be dashed to pieces
by its being carried without a Providence,
and so perish, and come to nought.
So that, by the forementioned predictions of Daniel,
those men seem to me very much to err from the truth,
who determine that God exercises no providence over human affairs;
for if that were the case, that the world went on by mechanical necessity,
we should not see that all things would come to pass
according to his prophecy.

Flavius Josephus

(Antiquities of the Jews, William Whiston translation, Book X, 11:7)

OTHER BOOKS BY C. S. MORRISON

Published works

THE BLIND MINDMAKER
Explaining Consciousness
without Magic or Misrepresentation

SURPRISED BY THE POWER OF DANIEL
The Miracles that brought a Skeptic to Faith

A RHYME, RHYMES AND HALF A RHYME
A Collection of Poems celebrating the Book of Daniel

Forthcoming works

THE WOW! SIGNAL
Hidden Evidence of an Intelligence
far more Advanced than Us